AF412526

AMERICA'S BIMODAL CRISIS:
BLACK INTELLIGENCE
IN
WHITE SOCIETY

Third Edition

by

Stanley Burnham

Foundation for Human Understanding
Athens, Georgia
1993

Contents

I

INTRODUCTION

L OW BLACK I.Q. AVERAGES persist as the most carefully guarded secret in the United States. For the
past forty years the same energies have been exerted
by the same assortment of scholars, experts, and opinion
makers to perpetuate this secret, and we may expect a
continuation of this effort into the foreseeable future. But
with few exceptions, I.Q. tests disclose virtually the same
cognitive differences as before despite the hundreds of
billions of dollars that have been spent to improve the
education and social status of blacks. Granted, many
blacks have benefitted from integrated schooling, and,
granted, many of them deserve the ample rewards that
have accrued from their education, but the gains of many
others have only been possible because of quotas
(euphemistically described as "diversity guidelines" or
"race norming") enforced by our courts and state and
federal bureaucracies. Meanwhile, black I.Q. and aptitude
test averages continue to be low, the average standard of
living among the black underclass has actually declined,

and, as has always been the case, black deprivation continues to be universal, not merely a unique blemish on American democracy.

Indeed there is no other society in the world, nor has there ever been one, in which black achievements in education and social progress measure up to European or North American standards. Nowhere else do blacks do any better. Almost the entire sub-Sahara African continent is a pitiful basket case, and so is Haiti, the oldest independent black society in the world. The rest of the black population in the Caribbean lives at a subsistence level, as does the large black minority in Brazil and the small urban black communities in Europe, which apparently suffer the same problems as their counterparts in American cities. Where else on the face of the earth does a black majority, or even a sizable black minority, enjoy a comfortable standard of living? Nowhere, as far as I can tell. As wide as the discrepancy seems today between black and white living standards in the United States, it is even wider between black living standards here in the United States and black living standards in Africa, South America, and the Caribbean region. Despite their inferior circumstances compared to their white compatriots, American blacks enjoy, on the average, the most advanced educational training, the best opportunity for upward mobility, and the most comfortable lifestyle of any sizable black community anywhere in the world in recorded history. Yet the relative deprivation of American blacks as compared to whites is treated as a uniquely disgraceful problem that can only be redressed if the white majority absorbs even bigger quotas and spends even more money on compensatory equal rights programs.

How did we ever burden ourselves with such an impossible goal? Quite simply, because black victimology has become a major American industry. Professional liberals and black spokespeople have incessantly hammered on the theme of white responsibility for black poverty, black crime, and black incompetence. In just about every instance, they claim, black shortcomings are the product of white prejudice (see Roth, 1990; Taylor, 1992). If blacks fail in schools, or abuse welfare, or procreate randomly, or engage in too much petty theft and violent crime, or cost too much government money, it is the fault of somebody else, not blacks themselves, since they would eagerly leap at the opportunity to join the white middle class if only given the chance. If blacks cannot find jobs because of their lack of qualifications, they are victimized because they have been unfairly isolated from the mainstream. But, if hired, they are victimized because they must be fired or demoted for incompetence, or because they are not promoted soon enough, or because they are not fully appreciated by their white coworkers, or because it is simply too much of a strain to cope with the white world. Somehow they are victimized. If white property owners sell at a loss and move elsewhere, it is the blacks that buy their houses at bargain prices who are victimized because they cannot escape the ghetto—it follows them wherever they go. And if white high school students retreat to private, parochial, or suburban schools to obtain an adequate education free of hooliganism and custodial school policies, it is the black students who are victimized because they cannot be adequately acculturated to succeed in later life. Even black muggers and rapists are somehow victimized by those whom they brutalize. Liberal apologists have been too sophisticated to present their case with rhetoric quite this simplistic, but this is pretty much their message as understood by most Americans today. It seems as if black inadequacy has achieved almost a teflon invulnerability to blame. Nothing is their own fault—it is always the fault of somebody else, anybody else.

The alternative explanation to be explored in this book—that nobody, exactly, is to blame, neither blacks nor whites—is based on the simple and demonstrable premise that the problems of the black community primarily result from a genetic deficiency in Negro intelligence as compared to the other races. In effect, our racial crisis in America today is the product of a significant bimodal gap that separates average black intelligence from the average intelligence of everybody else. Some blacks are every bit as intelligent as whites, but the great majority are not. If the average white I.Q. is approximately 100, while that of Jews and Orientals is somewhat higher and that of Mexicans and American Indians somewhat lower, that of the American Negro is significantly lower—approximately 15 points on the average, almost exactly an entire standard deviation (the average difference of a population from its mean). And the I.Q. of Africans of pure descent (without any Caucasian ancestors) turns out to be even lower—according to Lynn (1991a) as low as 80 in Ghana and Uganda, 75 in Nigeria, and 65 in the Congo (Zaire).

As first explained by Charles E. Spearman (1923) and later by Arthur Jensen (1980), I.Q. consists of the basic eductive capacity (identified as g) to generalize from examples, and, vice versa, to find evidence supportive of generalizations. Since this capacity lets one both associate and differentiate as well as draw conclusions and test assumptions based on these conclusions, it makes its presence felt in virtually every human activity from preparing supper to building skyscrapers and publishing variorum editions of Shakespeare. In one culture it might manifest itself in high productivity levels typical of the Protestant ethic, but in another it might take a different form, perhaps the ability to negotiate a transaction, or to obtain superior pasture lands, or even to appease neighbors and flatter tribal elders the most effectively. Those who possess a superior I.Q. will usually tend to benefit from it, while those who do not will usually tend to fall short. Of course, many exceptions may be found, but in general a higher I.Q. tends to improve one's circumstances, as may be demonstrated by the significant correlations that have been established between I.Q. and both socioeconomic status (Eells, 1951; Kemp, 1955) and the adequacy of one's job performance (Gottfredson, 1986).

Contrary to popular opinion, there is ample statistical data confirming racial differences in I.Q. Shuey (1966) and Osborne and McGurk (1982) have summarized in detail the many hundreds of studies that have confirmed an approximately 15-point deficiency in average I.Q. among American Negroes. Arthur Jensen summarizes this evidence in Chapter 6 of *Straight Talk About Mental Tests* (1981), as do Mark Snyderman and Stanley Rothman in *The I.Q Controversy: The Median and Public Policy* (1988), and Daniel Seligman in *The Question of Intelligence* (1992). Moreover, contrary to liberal claims, neither Wigdor and Garner (1982a, 1982b) nor Jensen in his monumental study of test bias, *Bias in Mental Testing* (1980), and in two of his subsequent articles (1985, 1987) found any evidence of cultural bias against blacks that was built into I.Q. testing. As of today there is no valid statistical evidence that any of these studies has been culturally loaded at the expense of blacks, and in fact black performance levels have been consistently the highest (albeit lower than whites) on the vocabulary and general information scales, supposedly the two particular scales the most likely to be biased by acculturation. Blacks perform by far the worst on scales the least likely to be influenced by cultural bias, for example in the comprehension of spatial relationships. Testing eductive quickness alone as a measure of I.Q., Jensen and others have measured simple choice reaction times (RT—the quickness with which simple cognitive decisions can be made) to confirm that even here black intelligence is slower than white intelligence (Jensen, 1980, 1982b; Eysenck, 1982; Ho, Baker and Decker, 1988; and Vernon, 1989). Useful recent summaries that survey the impressive accumulation of data and arguments pertaining to racial I.Q. differences include articles by Levin (1990, 1991) and Lynn (1991a, 1991b) as well as Snyderman and Rothman's *The IQ Controversy, the Media and Public Policy* (1988).

A contrary viewpoint is argued by Vincent (1991), who summarizes thirteen studies presumably demonstrating that black and white American children's I.Q. differences have been narrowed by approximately half during the 1980's. By comparing four pre-1980 studies with nine post-1980 studies, Vincent maintains that black-white I.Q. differences have appreciably declined in the last decade. However, the four pre-1980 studies are based on original norms, while four of the nine post-1980 studies use restandardized norms and in the other five studies the I.Q. scores are adjusted for socioeconomic status, allowing comparisons between different black and white sample test populations relative to their populations as a whole. That these pre- and post-1980 I.Q. comparisons somewhat differ should therefore come as no surprise. Meanwhile, the SAT averages of high school students continue to reflect almost a complete standard deviation difference between whites and blacks (Hacker, pp. 138, 142).

Numerous studies have also demonstrated the major role of genetic inheritance on I.Q.—anywhere between 60 percent and 80 percent. That one's environment plays a major role cannot be denied, but genetics apparently plays an even bigger role. During the seventies, Herrnstein and Eysenck claimed there is as much as an 80 percent dominance in favor of genetics. In his twin study, *Twins: Black and White* (1980), Osborne found a 66 percent dominance, and in Wilson and Herrnstein's *Crime and Human Nature* (1985) Herrnstein reduced his estimate to 60 percent. However, the more recent twins study of Bouchard *et al.* (1990) has once again increased the probable genetic input to as much as 70 percent. Whatever ratio is finally accepted, nobody today who has seriously explored the question gives environment a dominant role in the formation of I.Q. With rare exceptions, no miracles can be expected that significantly increase I.Q. by improving the family and social background of the individual, whether black or white.

Liberal apologists argue that there is no evidence to justify the emphasis upon genetics in explaining black I.Q., since the only measurable difference between the races consists of skin color. However, Chapter 4 lists numerous measurable biological differences, and recent studies by Rushton (1988a & b, 1989a, 1991b, etc.) augment the total with a variety of behavioral differences. But undoubtedly the most important racial variation bearing on racial I.Q. differences would be in brain size. Measurements by Ho *et al.* (1980a, 1980b, 1981) have established that the brains of American Negroes are approximately 8 percent smaller than those of whites, and this difference applies both in absolute size and in proportion to body weight. Roughly the same ratio was found by earlier studies listed in Chapter 4 and also by Beals *et al.* (1984), whose world-wide survey of 20,000 crania established the average brain case in Asia to contain 1380 cubic centimeters, in Europe, 1362, and in Africa, 1276. Based on these averages, the African brain is over 6 percent smaller than the European brain and over 7 percent smaller than the Asian brain. Other studies with comparable results are by Broman *et al.* (1987) and by Gordon *et al.* (1988), the latter based on the measurements of U. S. army personnel.

This 6 to 8 percent difference between blacks and whites in average brain size becomes important once the calculations of Van Valen (1974) that establish a .30 correlation between brain size and intelligence are taken into account. Willerman *et al.* (1989) and Jensen and Sinha (1991) have used magnetic resonance imaging to show an even higher correlation of .35, and Lynn (1991b) has summarized the literature bearing on this correlation and has offered a possible evolutionary explanation for it. Also supportive of these conclusions are papers by Lynn (1990) and Rushton (1990a and b). Despite the strenuous efforts of Stephen Jay Gould (1981), Cain and Vanderwolf (1990), and others to reject this data, there is now an overwhelming preponderance of evidence that blacks probably do have smaller brains than whites and that relative brain size probably does bear a strong positive correlation with I.Q. Therefore, as explained in Chapter 4, the cognitive deficiency of blacks can very likely be linked with their smaller brain sizes.

Earlier studies also discussed in Chapter 4 likewise suggest the possibility of more dramatic structural differences between black and white brains, primarily in the prefrontal region where cognitive thinking takes place. Here black brain sizes might be as much as 12 percent smaller than comparable portions of white brains. Since the cerebral cortex plays an inhibitory role with lower brain centers, it may be suggested that an imbalance favorable to these lower brain centers very likely produces significant variations in conscious behavior additional to the burden of cognitive deficiency. Greater restlessness may be anticipated, as well as heightened aggressiveness, quicker emotions, better rhythm and coordination, a more active libido, etc. On one hand there would be less capacity for cognitive performance, and on the other hand more emotional "noise" to distract the mind from engaging in this performance. This relative imbalance perhaps helps to explain many of the behavioral differences emphasized by Rushton as well as the "time-preference differences" Michael Levin (1991) finds in the tendency among many blacks to favor immediate impulse at the expense of long-range goals.

When an individual possesses a low I.Q., his inadequacies may be anticipated and absorbed by society at large, usually by limiting his employment to tasks he can cope with. This social flexibility in dealing with cognitively disadvantaged individuals may be observed on a universal basis. But what happens if the majority of a population or sub-population suffers from this deficiency? What if there are too few competent individuals to provide the leadership and consensus of responsible opinion for an adequate social and political infrastructure to emerge? Here a more pervasive pattern of social dysfunction may be anticipated, and, indeed, the circumstances of the black community throughout the world almost exactly fit the pattern to be expected for groups generally deficient in I.Q. If anthropologists and sociologists could devise a statistical model for predicting the collective behavior of populations and sub-populations with an average I.Q. of 85 or lower, how would this model significantly differ from the primitive circumstances in Africa before its European colonization (as surveyed in Chapter 6), or from its collapse subsequent to the departure of the colonial infrastructures (as surveyed in Chapter 7), or from the chronic poverty of the American ghetto (as surveyed in Chapters 8 and 9)? In all three instances, what might be described as an utterly impoverished lifestyle has prevailed that has frequently lapsed into anarchy and social disruption. As Levin insists, "The absence of evidence favorable to equality is, in this instance, evidence against it." (1991, p. 196).

It is again to be conceded that many blacks are fully as intelligent as the white majority, but their proportional representation at any level of intelligence among our nation's potentially effective leadership is more than four to one favorable to whites. For example, only 2.3 percent of blacks have at least 115 I.Q.'s as compared to 16 percent of whites, and only a fraction of 1 percent of blacks have at least 127 I.Q.'s as compared to 4 percent of whites. In the United States, in which the black population is approximately 12 percent of the whole, this means that well more than thirty times as many whites as blacks can draw on the minimal eductive skills needed for any particular occupation, for example, as doctors, lawyers, or corporate executives—a discrepancy that can only augment the anger and frustration of both the black and white communities—the former because they have been brainwashed by liberal rhetoric to demand a bigger share of the upscale job market, and the latter as long as "race norming" is used to impose compensatory representation for black employees at all levels of achievement regardless of obvious bimodal differences in ability levels (see Blits and Gottfredson, 1990a and 1990b; Epstein, 1992). If the population size of the black minority is steadily increasing as a proportion of the total U. S. population by a half percent per decade (Hacker, p. 15), the prospects of a much bigger problem loom in the future, and one can only be pessimistic of our nation's prospects.

The mounting social dysfunction in our nation's black community that culminated in the 1992 Los Angeles riots has been amply explored by a variety of excellent studies published within the last decade. As argued by Jared Taylor in his recent book, *Paved with Good Intentions* (1992), a black underclass does exist in the United States as demonstrated by virtually every statistical category: the remarkable average that one-quarter of all black males in their twenties are in jail, on parole, or on probation—ten times the rate for white males of the same age; the no less remarkable average that blacks commit more than half of all the rapes and robberies and more than 60 percent of all the murders though they comprise only 12 percent of the total population; a homicide rate for blacks that has increased by two-thirds since 1983; a diminishing life expectancy for black males between fifteen and twenty-four for each of the last five years because of homicides; a syphilis rate fifty times as high for blacks as for whites; an infant mortality rate twice as high for blacks as for whites; a poverty rate for black children four times as high as for whites; an illegitimacy rate for blacks now more than 66 percent as compared to 19 percent for whites; an unemployment rate for black youth twice as high as for whites; a median net worth for black families only $3,397, less than one-eleventh of that for the average white family; and a dependency on public assistance four and a half times as high as for whites. As explained by Taylor, "Just one or two of these numbers would be evidence of a nation gone wrong. Taken together, they are a catastrophe—and in the time since they were collected, many have gotten worse" (pp. 10–11).

In *Losing Ground: American Social Policy 1950–1980* (1984), Charles Murray proposes the controversial thesis that the American welfare establishment has contributed to this social dysfunction in the black community by imposing a variety of family and social dislocations that have forced the black community into a dependency role. Murray's thesis has been severely criticized by liberal apologists, but anybody at either end of the welfare system—welfare workers and their clients—will gladly explain in detail, once guaranteed confidentiality, how welfare encourages the breakup of the family and the demoralization of everybody involved. This was explained to me by a young man, now on Workman's Compensation because of a serious injury, who was encouraged to get divorced, then "get lost," so as to obtain free Medicaid and adequate subsidized housing for his family. Here I directly quote his remarks word for word over the telephone as I am typing:

What we end up with is a situation where families are forced into disintegration in order to receive benefits, and welfare workers expect the head of the household to cheat and at the same time make it clear that if he is caught cheating he will be kicked out of the system. This leaves the children not only economically deprived but provided with no positive male role model—and a female role model reduced to depending on deception in order to survive.

Male adolescents who want to escape from such households merely need to shift their loyalty to neighborhood gangs, while female adolescents may exercise the option of getting pregnant either to supplement their mothers' incomes or to start comparable households of their own— poor households, but their own. For individuals who belong to the white majority such an arrangement is disorienting, and for the growing underclass of whites it bears an obviously harmful impact. But for an entire subculture of blacks resentful of white hegemony the present welfare system can only intensify the severe antisocial disorientation already aggravated by their inadequate cognitive skills. When liberal apologists try to argue otherwise they do not know what they are talking about.

Other useful books about the current black crisis include Nicholas Lehmann's *The Promised Land* (1991), an account of the black migration from the south to northern cities since the end of World War II; William Wilson's *The Truly Disadvantaged* (1987), an explanation of how the departure of the black middle class from the ghetto has further aggravated the crisis by depriving the ghetto of its normal leadership; Mark Snyderman and Stanley Rothman's *The IQ Controversy, the Media and Public Policy* (1988), an account of the extreme public bias against "racist" scientific information; Roger Pearson's *Race, Intelligence and Bias in Academe* (1991), an account of the academic pressure to discourage valid speculation about racial differences; Thomas and Mary Edsall's *Chain Reaction: The Impact of Race, Rights, and Taxes on American Politics* (1991), an explanation of how the Democratic Party's emphasis upon black needs cost it its middle class majority and forced it into an uneasy client relationship with a variety of PACs; and James Wilson and Richard Herrnstein's *Crime and Human Nature* (1985), a treatment of the genetic makeup of criminals, both black and white. It may be mentioned here that Michael Levin's article, "Responses to Race Differences in Crime" (1992), is also useful as a theoretical treatment of probabilities in dealing with black criminal behavior.

Two other books worthy of mention are Christopher Jencks' *Rethinking Social Policy: Race, Poverty, and the Underclass* (1992) and Andrew Hacker's *Two Nations: Black and White, Separate, Hostile, Unequal* (1992). Both Jencks and Hacker necessarily take a liberal viewpoint, but the manner in which they hedge their arguments helps to document the present understanding of the issue among our nation's leadership. Jencks tries to argue both sides of the case, and some of his distinctions are genuinely insightful, while Hacker resorts to liberal cant without always adequately double checking his information. Nevertheless, he documents his case with numerous statistical tables that effectively indicate the extent of the black crisis regardless of its cause. As a result, his tables are just as useful to geneticists as to environmentalists in demonstrating the problems that need to be addressed. Both Jencks and Hacker descend to ignorant, almost laughable, rationalizations when they discuss I.Q. and the issue of heredity—Jencks on pages 104–7 and Hacker on pages 26–28—but one may assume that this was necessary to obtain the publication of their books by the orthodox trade press. Amusingly, Hacker (p. 24) also evokes Thomas Jefferson's words, "that all men are created equal", to challenge the mounting suspicion among many today of black genetic inferiority in I.Q. Apparently Hacker is unaware of Jefferson's arguments in Query 14 of his *Notes on the State of Virginia*, published in 1781, to the effect that "blacks . . . are inferior to the whites in the endowments both of body and mind" and that "differences in fixed nature" (which Jefferson describes in detail) provide "a powerful obstacle to the emancipation of these people." (Jefferson, pp. 264–270). Nobody today would want to deprive blacks of their civil and social rights, but such figures as Jefferson should be used cautiously by liberal apologists to support their claims.

My own opinion at this point is that race is probably our nation's most urgent problem, and that chances are strong we shall ultimately be consumed by it. As Joseph Tainter has amply demonstrated (1988), all societies eventually lose their competitive edge and fall into decline, and in the case of the United States, I suspect, race will continue to play its role as one of the primary sources of such an outcome. Arnold Toynbee's notion of challenge and response would posit our crisis in race relations as our most basic challenge to surmount, but, as almost everybody realizes, we simply are not doing it. Here, I think, the most radical black activists would agree with both liberals and geneticists. What the Los Angeles riots demonstrated more than anything else, in my opinion, was the utter bankruptcy of federal programs for dealing with race relations. They simply have not worked, and I believe the principal reason for this has been the implementation of misguided programs justified by grotesque misinformation, much of which results from the calculated neglect of I.Q. differences.

During the seventies there was a liberal agenda based on the supposition that the racial issue could be resolved simply by spending sufficient amounts of money. Be generous enough and wear down white resistance hard enough, and the black underclass will merge with the white middle class—this was the common assumption shared by almost everybody who played a role in running our country. When Reagan came to power, this strategy could be rejected as having been a failure, so it was tabled in favor of a new perception that the best policy was one of benign neglect. Our priorities would accordingly shift to economic incentives presumably beneficial to all Americans on the assumption that a general rise in our standard of living would extend to blacks as well. It turns out, of course, that neither strategy worked. And the failure of both, I think, derives from the shared assumption that black inadequacy can be dealt with on an orthodox economic basis.

Quite the contrary, in my opinion, our racial crisis is intractable and cannot be "solved." Its source is ultimately genetic, not environmental, so it cannot be bought off. There is no way to pay for its elimination. The best way to deal with it is as if it were a chronic disease—like malaria—one that must always be treated but cannot be entirely cured. The liberals of the seventies were correct that enormous federal funding is needed, but the conservatives of the eighties were also correct that this funding cannot be expected to produce miraculous results. In effect, lots of money must be spent, but without any anticipation of producing significant improvement. The best we can expect is to minimize social decline, and a large portion of our energies and national income will always be needed for this purpose. Integrationist priorities must be sustained for those blacks able and willing to take advantage of them, but our schools cannot continue to be misused as enlightened detention centers, dysfunctional families cannot continue to be spawned by misguided state and federal programs, our businesses and government agencies cannot continue to be overstaffed by marginally competent individuals, and our criminal justice system cannot continue to be squandered to guarantee the constitutional rights of an army of young hoodlums otherwise indifferent to the law. Somehow, a *de facto* two-track arrangement must be devised in all these areas to accommodate black needs at a basic subsistence level independent of our mainstream culture and economy, yet flexible enough to accommodate those many blacks able and willing to make the transition into the main stream on a truly competitive basis. Blacks in the first group would of course be provided make-work sources of income, and blacks in the second group would of course be given the needed compensatory education to adjust to a truly color-free marketplace for jobs and services. Can such an arrangement be devised under our present system of government and with our present collective ideological commitments? I doubt it, but our only chance of survival as a nation depends on making such an effort. Otherwise, we join the third world within the next few decades.

So there is nothing to regret in my revision of *Black Intelligence in White Society*, first published in 1985. But I want to emphasize that I take no pleasure in the information summarized here. If Vincent's findings about recent improvements in the measured average I.Q. of middle-class black children bear any value in predicting further improvements, I would be entirely delighted. However, too much evidence has been gathered to suggest otherwise, and the use of sample populations seems flawed in the experiments surveyed by Vincent. So I am not convinced. Nor do I seek any compensation for my authorship or anticipate any professional privileges or recognition as would be suggested by my use of a pseudonym. If and when my identity is discovered by my colleagues, I can expect to be forced into early retirement, probably within the month. My only reason for writing this book is my concern that the truth in race relations has been too effectively suppressed, and at a potential cost that might be catastrophic for our society as a whole.

Have I always advocated what might be described as a racist position? Not at all. Through high school my politics were those of a conservative Republican (actually a "Taft Republican") with strong sympathies for the black cause, and when I reached college I became a liberal, then a campus radical—a Marxist, actually—and, of course, with even stronger sympathies for the black cause. It was only when I spent two years teaching English in an inner city junior college, then another two years educating inner city secondary school teachers, then another three years living in what might be described as a transitional neighborhood that I began to realize our nation is up against a much more difficult task than I had previously recognized. My children's attendance in three different inner city high schools also reinforced this insight, as did my observation of black students over a couple of decades of teaching. It is because of these experiences that I vigorously differ on the race question with individuals with whom I otherwise agree on many social and cultural issues. I am confident that if they could have shared the same experiences they would also be able to share my sense of urgency that the facts now suppressed by the liberal establishment must be publicized to help awaken our nation to its present crisis. I have no doubt that my words here will be read and appreciated a century from now; I only hope that they can help bring some of the needed changes within the next decade or two.

II

PSYCHOMETRIC DATA

THE SO-CALLED NORMAL BELL-SHAPED CURVE was discovered by Sir Francis Galton to measure performance levels for just about any kind of behavior, including intelligence. An average score (or mean) could be calculated (for example, the I.Q. of 100), and roughly 68 percent of the total scores could be expected to fall within the average distance from this average score. This average distance from the average (or mean) is called the standard deviation (or SD), and for a normal distribution with a percentile range of 0 to 100, the SD generally falls between the 16th and 84th percentiles. For the average I.Q. of the American population as a whole this range extends between the scores of 85 and 115. However, if two separate populations are measured on the same scale; for example, in calculating the height or running speed of men and women, then what is described as a BIMODAL DISTRIBUTION may be detected by which two normal curves overlap based on separate averages and standard deviations for the two distinct groups. The overall difference between these two normal curves may thus be calculated based on the SD percentage between the two respective averages (or means). For example, if 50 percent of the men run faster than 84 percent of the women, then an entire standard deviation separates the two groups. Such is the case, it turns out, for the spatial perception scales in I.Q. tests, which produce a male average just about an entire SD higher than the female average. However, female averages exceed male averages on all other I.Q. scales well enough to offset this advantage, so the overall average I.Q. is virtually identical for men and women. The two average I.Q. profiles are different, but as a sum total the average I.Q. turns out to be the same for both sexes.

However, this is not the case for the bimodal distribution between black and white I.Q.'s, since no scales sufficiently offset other scales to erase what amounts to virtually an entire standard deviation between the two overall averages. Like women, blacks score the lowest on spatial perception and arithmetic scales, but though they score higher on vocabulary and general information scales (supposedly the most culturally "biased" in the battery of I.Q. tests), their total scores on all scales add up to be significantly lower than for whites, both male and female. In fact, their total I.Q. average remains just about an entire standard deviation below the average for whites, and, whatever the cause, genetic or environmental, nothing has been found in psychometric theory to eliminate this difference. Moreover, the black normal distribution is somewhat narrower because its variance is only three-quarters of that for whites (meaning that there are even fewer geniuses than would be indicated by the normal-curve differences); and, in contrast to the parity between the sexes for whites, black female I.Q. averages tend to be four to five points higher than for black males. Despite extraordinary efforts by psychometricians, no verifiably unbiased test has been devised to eliminate these differences and bring black averages in line with white averages. Thus, over 50 percent of our black population have I.Q.'s less than 85, only 16 percent have I.Q.'s higher than 100, only 2.3 percent have I.Q.'s higher than 115 as compared to 16 percent of whites, and only a minuscule tenth of a percent have I.Q.'s higher than 130 as compared to 2.3 percent of whites. (See Figure 1). As a result, our nation suffers from what can be described as a BIMO-DAL CRISIS in race relations, since this difference in cognitive ability is big enough to have led to very major social problems that have only been aggravated by the vigorous effort over the last five decades to deny their existence.

Literally hundreds of experiments have been conducted to confirm this bimodal discrepancy between black and white averages on I.Q. tests. As many as 750 of these experiments were summarized by Audrey Shuey (1966) in her neglected classic survey, *The Testing of Negro Intelligence*, as well as by Osborne and McGurk (1982) in their co-authored supplement, updated sixteen years later. Each of these volumes provides a comprehensive summary of experimentation up to its date of publication, and almost all the data they have gathered (with no exclusions due to editorial bias) compellingly supports the conclusion that the average black I.Q. in the United States is approximately 15 points below the white average, and that at least ten of these points may be chalked up to genetics alone, independent of environmental factors. Neither of these two volumes has been refuted or

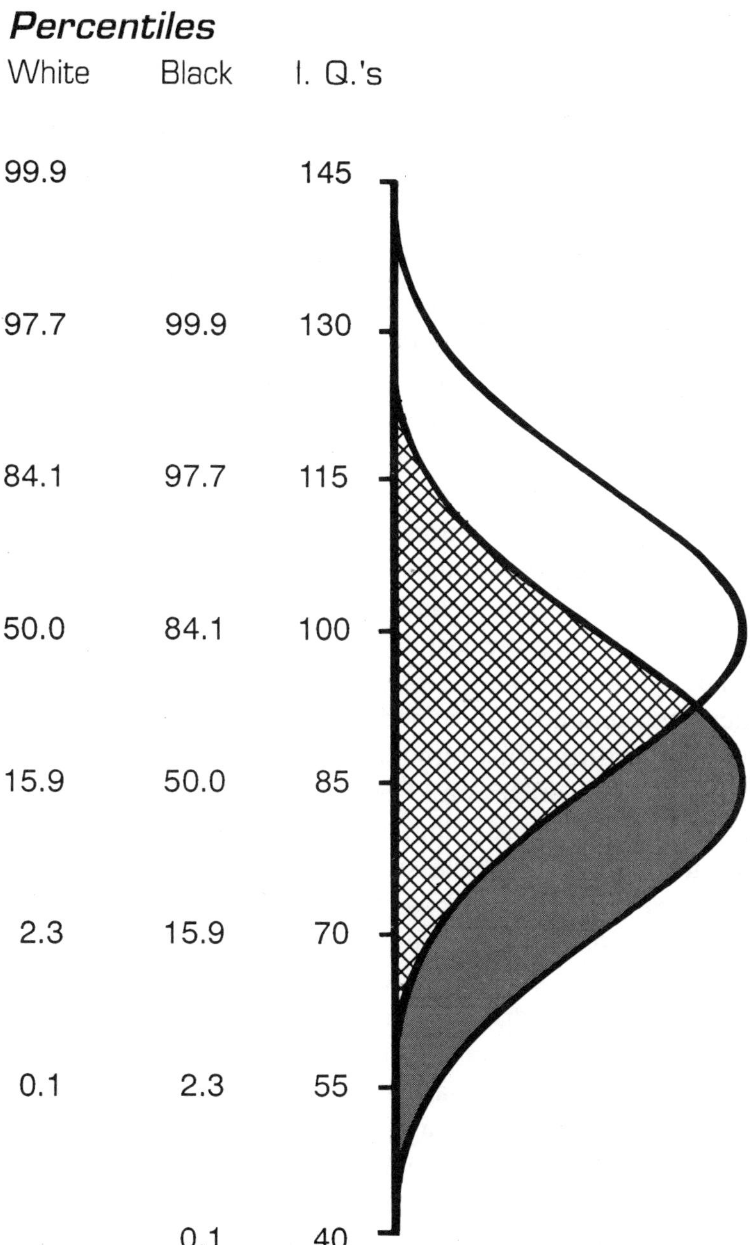

Figure 1: *Overlapping normal curves showing white and black I. Q. distributions and percentile ranks for I. Q.'s in each distribution.*

even mentioned by the liberal press, apparently on the assumption that what is best ignored should be obliterated from the public record. Nevertheless, Shuey's encyclopedic survey and its equally encyclopedic supplement by Osborne and McGurk give us an accurate and thorough-going perspective of interracial I.Q. testing, and the wide range of experiments they have summarized provides considerable valid scientific data in support of racial differences. Whether the public knows it or not, there is an entire field of scientific inquiry with an enormous accumulation of verified data almost all of which confirms the Jensenist argument.

It should also be stressed that most interracial I.Q. experiments conducted over the last decade or two have included elaborate precautions to minimize test bias that might result from differences in cultural background. To reduce, if not eliminate, a built-in cultural bias against blacks, dozens of relatively culture-free experiments have been devised, but it has been found, paradoxically, that the least biased of these tests have produced the biggest measurable differences. The greater the culture-loading on particular I.Q. scales, the better blacks perform; the smaller the culture-loading, the worse they perform. In one of the most dramatic experiments to prove this thesis, by Jensen and R. A. Figueroa (1975), forward and backwards digit-span I.Q. tests were given to black and white subjects from comparable socioeconomic backgrounds. For the forward digit-span component of the test, measuring both short-term memory and one's general familiarity with numbers, blacks scored a relatively modest .25 standard deviation less than whites, indicating somewhat comparable ability in both recognizing and recalling sequences of numbers. However, for the backwards digit-span component of the test, additionally measuring the limited cognitive skills needed to transpose digits one at a time in reverse sequence (431 becoming 134), this difference more than doubled to become a .57 SD between the races. Apparently, blacks were almost as adept at remembering numbers as whites, but not as competent in reversing their positions one at a time from the last number to the first. Their familiarity with numbers proved to be almost the same as for whites, but not their ability to manipulate numbers according to arbitrary guidelines (in this instance the reversal of sequence). They knew as much, but they could not do as much with what they knew.

It is to be acknowledged that a handful of the interracial I.Q. experiments summarized by Shuey and Osborne & McGurk indicates a smaller difference than a full standard deviation between black and white I.Q. averages, but these few experiments may be discounted either because they depended upon an uneven selectivity of sample populations [for example, with Otto Klineberg (1935, 1944) and Ashley Montague's (1945) inexcusable misuse of First World War I.Q. data, as explained by Shuey (1966)] or because accidental results were obtained that cannot be confirmed by further testing. For example, Rosenthal and Jacobson's (1968) razzle-dazzle proof of a "Pygmalion Effect" in improved performance levels produced by glowing teachers' expectations has collapsed upon further experimentation. Otherwise, the ample data gathered over the last several decades has overwhelmingly supported the probability of a chronic built-in 15-point difference between black and white I.Q. averages. These results have likewise been confirmed by national SAT averages finally released in 1979 by a House of

Representatives subcommittee after seven years of effective "affirmative" censorship (i.e., suppression in the service of a benevolent cause). Nationwide since the tests began, whites averaged 455 on the verbal scale as compared to 336 for blacks, and 493 on the mathematics scale as compared to 359 for blacks. Since 100 points represent a single standard deviation on the SAT (equal to 15 points in I.Q.), blacks once again scored the equivalent of at least fifteen I.Q. points behind their white classmates. This difference seems to have been even greater at the top of the scale: of the 9,128 students nationwide whose SAT scores exceeded 700 in the year 1983, only 66 were black, a tiny .7 percent of the total (i.e., seven-tenths of one percent). As in the case with I.Q., the right slope of the normal curve measuring superior performance among blacks tapered off much more rapidly than among whites. What are the SAT discrepancies today between black and white high school students? As compared to the combined verbal and mathematical averages in 1979 of 948 for whites and 695 for blacks (with a 200 point SD), the combined averages in 1990, eleven years later, were respectively 933 for whites and 737 for blacks, so, despite extraordinary effort on the part of our educational establishment, the gap has been narrowed by only 57 points and virtually an entire SD continues to separate the two populations (Hacker, p. 142). It seems that only by blurring test results with various procedures that demonstrably bias scoring in favor of blacks can we expect to narrow the gap to any appreciable extent.

The wide difference in I.Q. between the races has likewise been confirmed by Osborne's 1980 study already mentioned which was based on the exhaustive statistical investigation of almost five hundred sets of twins. By far the most comprehensive twins study yet, it once again lends credence to Jensen's thesis, this time with results which confirm a genetic basis for I.Q. differences between the races. Additional confirmation came from the New York City Police Department when it took extraordinary steps to devise a supposedly bias-free examination to establish the graded eligibility of patrolmen for promotion to sergeants. Instead of asking the usual questions for determining verbal and quantitative skills, testers presented filmed dramatizations of everyday encounters on the job and asked a variety of questions pertaining to what happened and what could be done about it. Administered in June, 1984, the test bore results which once again demonstrated the cognitive inferiority of blacks by as much as a full standard deviation: 10.6 percent of the white candidates passed the test as compared to only 1.4 percent of the black candidates. Unfortunately, the egalitarian supposition universally held as an article of faith by liberals is supported by almost no psychometric data of its own. It floats free and clear of the tasks of statistical verification.

III

THE VERIFICATION OF
PSYCHOMETRIC DATA

THE NOTION of an inevitable culture bias built into I.Q. tests has become one of the most hallowed assumptions of liberal doctrine, but in fact racial bias has been virtually eliminated from I.Q. testing through a variety of complex statistical verification procedures. In his monumental 786-page study, *Bias in Mental Testing* (1980), Arthur Jensen devotes unprecedented analysis and probably unmatched statistical sophistication to the study of those verification procedures which give I.Q. testing high validity as an indication of racial differences. Jensen's effort can be praised as a major contribution to statistical theory in demonstrating, (a) that factor analysis may be used to isolate and verify the existence of basic eductive skills as measured by I.Q., (b) that cultural bias may be accurately measured and thus eliminated in I.Q. testing among comparative populations, and (c) that cultural bias can thus be discounted as a cause of I.Q. differences between black and white sample populations. Jensen also confirms that black performance levels have been the highest on so-called culture-biased tests such as for vocabulary and general information, but have plummeted on so-called culture-free tests, especially those which measure skills in computation and spatial configuration.

Jensen's primary contribution in *Bias in Mental Testing* is his establishment of statistical procedures to determine the degree of culture bias for particular cultures, sub-cultures and nationalities. The procedures he outlines clearly demonstrate the likelihood of culture bias in the testing of Mexicans, Indians, and Orientals, for whom language difficulties continue to produce measurably lower scores. However, these procedures confirm the validity of low test results for black sample groups, if anything, exposing a test bias slightly too much in their favor. Not surprisingly, different races seem to produce different I.Q. averages, so it would be a mistake to surmise that there is a white supremacist bias in Jensen's approach to psychometrics. Though Jensen finds that Caucasians excel Negroes in I.Q. averages by fifteen points, he discloses that whites fall short of both Jews and Orientals, in the latter instance despite their statistically significant disadvantage in trying to cope with the English language.

As far as I can gather from Jensen's publications as well as my private correspondence with him, these are the I.Q. averages he finds among different races in the United States:

Jews	109	unbiased
Orientals	102–3	biased
Caucasians	100	unbiased
Mexicans and Indians	94–96	biased
Blacks	85	unbiased

Obviously, raw I.Q. averages are inaccurate to the extent that bias can be detected by means of statistical verification procedures, as seems to be the case for Orientals, Mexicans, and Indians. However, I.Q. testers are safeguarded from drawing the wrong conclusions by these statistical verification procedures which establish both the likelihood of bias and the degree to which it distorts the test results. In the case of blacks, there is no apparent bias indicated by these procedures. Their I.Q. averages fall far behind those of everybody else, and with absolutely no statistical evidence for treating culture bias as the cause of their lower scores.

Jensen's analysis is thorough and often incredibly abstruse in *Bias in Mental Testing* (1980), so the intelligent lay reader might profit from turning to Jensen's summary of his conclusions in his following book, *Straight Talk about Mental Tests* (1981), in which he addresses most of the common liberal misconceptions about I.Q. testing. For the best comprehensive survey of serious professional response to Jensen's contribution among reputable experts in the field of psychometrics, one may also turn to the colloquium published in *The Behavioral and Brain Sciences* (Harnad, 1980), which includes two dozen brief but technically accurate judgments by established psychometricians. Some participants attack specific applications of Jensen's statistical model, but most acknowledge his monumental contribution to psychometric theory. Other basic references which reinforce Jensen's conclusions include H. J. Eysenck's *The Inequality of Man* (1973), R. J. Herrnstein's *I.Q. in the Meritocracy* (1973), Loehlin, Lindzey and Spuhler's *Race Differences in Intelligence* (1975), and Philip Vernon's *Intelligence: Heredity and Environment* (1979). Obviously, Jensen does not stand alone on this issue, for there is an entire segment of psychometricians—perhaps a majority—who support his thesis.

Public ignorance of this development in the professional literature has been sustained only through a vigorous public relations campaign by quasi-scientific journalists willing to defend our liberal mythology by distorting current developments in psychometrics. While most professional journals in the field essentially support the Jensenist position, our liberal press willfully disregards this development and instead makes scapegoats of particular individuals (for example William Shockley and Cyril Burt) on an *ad hominem* basis. Any reference to the valid scientific findings of Jensen, Eysenck, Herrnstein, and Osborne is minimized, and irrelevant questions are emphasized instead of the basic issues under consideration. The two most publicized figures giving scientific respectability to this black whitewash, Leon Kamin and Stephen Jay Gould, wrote hostile popular reviews of Jensen's book *Bias in Mental Testing*, the former in *Psychology Today* and the latter in *The New York Review of Books*, but each of their reviews studiously neglected the most important arguments made by Jensen, and Gould in particular seems to have been entirely out of his depth with statistical theory. In *The Mismeasure of Man* (1981), Gould made ten brief allusions to Jensen, but they were all marred by obvious confusion and a basic misunderstanding of the material, as exposed by Jensen himself with painstaking thoroughness in his counter-review, "The Debunking of Scientific Fossils and Straw Persons," in *Contemporary Education Review* (1982a). Gould's effort to demonstrate the social bias at the root of nineteenth century anthropology obviously applies with equal and even more damaging validity to his own strategy, since most of the errors he exposed have long since been rectified. Every science begins with assumptions and procedures potentially susceptible to ridicule, but its initial mistakes should not be exaggerated to denigrate the importance of its subsequent discoveries, as Gould obviously tries to do despite the plenitude of valid evidence he can only deal with by ignoring.

According to Bernard Davis in "Neo-Lysenkoism, IQ, and the Press" (1983), Gould's effort to fit science to liberal doctrine bears obvious comparison with the effort of the notorious Soviet biologist Lysenko to confirm a Stalinist theory of social adaptation on a totally environmentalist basis. In his answer to Davis's review, Gould (1984) took exception to the epithet "Neo-Lysenkoist," but in fact his cavalier rejection of genetics as a major source of I.Q. discrepancies betrays a similar willingness to manipulate scientific objectivity in the service of egalitarian ideology. In both instances a radical environmentalist commitment has led to dangerous misconstructions based on the willful misinterpretation of valid data, and, of course, both Gould and Lysenko have linked their environmentalist bias with officially sanctioned programs of social modification—in Lysenko's case the Stalinist version of proletarian achievement, in Gould's case the equal opportunity programs implemented by our government since the mid-sixties. Each has been willing to sacrifice scientific accuracy to his own version of idealism, and for each there will probably be reserved an unsavory niche in the history of pseudo-scientific resistance to valid biological discovery.

IV

DIFFERENCES IN BODY AND BRAIN MEASUREMENTS

ANOTHER LIBERAL MISCONCEPTION has been the supposedly near-perfect physical resemblance between
the races except for skin coloration. There is no difference here, argue the egalitarian apologists, beyond super-
ficial pigmentation resulting from differences in sun
exposure. The more direct the sunlight, the greater the abundance of melanin in the skin, eyes, and hair to help protect
the body from excess radiation, but otherwise we are entirely
the same. However, it turns out that skin color is only one
among a wide array of physical differences between
blacks and whites, as catalogued by Frederick Hulse in
*The Human Species: An Introduction to Physical Anthro-
pology* (1963), by J. C. Carothers in *The Mind of Man in
Africa* (1972), by John Baker in *Race* (1974), and, more
briefly, by Jensen in *Straight Talk About Mental Tests*
(1981) in a passage which may be quoted in its entirety:

> A few of the many physical characteristics found to dis-
> play genetic variation between different races are body size

and proportions, hair forms and distribution, head shape and facial features, cranial capacity and brain formation, blood types, number of vertebras, size of genitalia, bone density, fingerprints, number and distribution of sweat glands, odor, consistency of ear wax, number of teeth, length of gestation period, frequency of twin births, male-female birth ratio, physical maturity at birth, rate of infant development of alpha brain waves, colorblindness, visual and auditory acuity, intolerance of milk, galvanic skin resistance, chronic diseases, susceptibility to infectious diseases, genetic diseases (e.g., Tay Sachs, sickle cell anemia), and pigmentation of the skin, hair, and eyes.

To continue the list, the eyeballs of blacks average about 9 percent larger, their ears are smaller, their nostrils wider, and their teeth more protruding than for whites. Until recently it was fashionable to insist that exactly the same blood courses through the veins of both blacks and whites, but studies since World War II have disclosed complex blood-group systems whose allele frequencies disclose the racial origins of a blood sample with excellent accuracy. In particular, the alleles R^o and $R^{o'}$ indicate the effectiveness of the Sahara Desert as a "gene-flow" barrier, since the incidence of this allele is in excess of 50 percent below the Sahara, but one-third or less above the Sahara. Individuals of African ancestry may also be differentiated by the absence of the U and Fy^b antigens as well as by an abundance of the Hb^s allele associated with sickle-cell hemoglobin. Since allele frequencies primarily result from the exposure of ancestors to particular diseases, differences in blood group systems serve to confirm the relative isolation of specific races over the last few thousand years. What is proven by these variations is that many biological differences do, in fact, exist between blacks and whites, even though variable blood-group statistics otherwise bear no relationship to I.Q., personality, or any other behavioral tendency.

Probably the most important variation between the races involves the size and structure of the brain, since Lee Van Valen has established as much as a .30 correlation between I.Q. and brain size in his useful 1974 article, "Brain Size and Intelligence in Man." Significant differences exist in brain size between the races, so it seems entirely feasible that I.Q. differences might result from them. According to J. C. Carothers in *The Mind of Man in Africa* (1972), only four studies have been conducted in which brain size was measured for comparison among black and white skulls on a consistent methodological basis. Mostly because of liberal disapproval, this kind of experimentation has been virtually abandoned subsequent to 1950. Its findings and rationale have been conveniently forgotten, first on the assumption that brain size cannot be correlated with intelligence, and later, once valid experiments had been forgotten, on the assumption that no such differences in size exist between the races. Nevertheless, in the four studies listed by Carothers, Negro brain size was established to be significantly smaller, averaging from 2.6 percent to 7.9 percent less than white brain size:

Study	Total number of brains measured	White average		Black average		Black average as % of white average
		Male	Female	Male	Female	
Todd (1923)	302	1391cc	1232	1350	1221	97.4
Pearl (1934)	403	1471	—	1355	—	92.1
Simmons (1942)	2241	1571	1339	1467	1311	97 appx.
Connolly (1950)	105	1288	1226	1198	1127	92.9

Obviously the most important column is the last one on the right. Sexual differences are unimportant since women's brains are smaller than men's on an absolute scale, but larger proportional to their body size. The relative variability in results may likewise be discounted partly because of the different groups measured (Connolly having compared Germans and American Negroes, Pearl having based his data on Civil War autopsies, etc.) and partly because of difficulties which result from the soft consistency of brain tissue (roughly comparable to peanut butter) and from the inaccessibility of the skull cavity. As to be expected, each study used different procedures in measuring brain size, but consistent procedures were applied to each skull regardless of race. Because the measurement of brain size necessarily varies depending upon these procedures, the wide variation in results among these four experiments is less important than their consistency in differentiating black and white averages somewhere in the range between two percent and eight percent in favor of whites.

Subsequent to Carothers' book, Khang-cheng Ho and associates published three articles, "Analysis of Brain Weight," I (1980a) and II (1980b), and "Newborn Brain Weight in Relation to Maturity, Sex, and Race" (1981), in which racial differences in brain size were again established on a statistical basis, and this time very careful procedures were used in conducting the measurements. Having measured 1,261 adult subjects (811 whites and 450 blacks) at the Case Western Institute of Psychology, Ho and his associates found a 106 gram difference in averages of black and white men (1,286 gm. versus 1,392 gm.) and a 94 gram difference in averages between black and white women (1,158 gm. versus 1,252 gm.). In other words, the brains of white men were 8.2 percent bigger than those of black men, and the brains of white women 8.1 percent bigger than those of black women. Ho and his associates found no statistically significant difference between the races (or between the sexes) for 782 newborn infants at the time of birth, and therefore concluded that adult differences must be chalked up to environmental conditioning. However, this explanation was offered as pure conjecture, and indeed the 9 percent difference between the sexes which comes with full growth despite their equal sizes at birth might bear its counterpart in the more than 8 percent difference which emerges between the races. An 8 percent difference seems far too big to be explained away on a strictly environmental basis, and, in fact, genetics probably affects the extent of post-natal brain development as much as it affects brain development during the early stages in utero. This is certainly the case for the differences that emerge between the sexes, and it seems no less likely for the differences that emerge between the races. Whatever the cause, the Ho data suggests that the brains of white adults are significantly bigger than those of black adults—even more than had been indicated by the earlier studies featured by Carothers.

Perhaps more important than brain-size differences are differences in brain shape, including the development of the cortex and frontal lobes, fissuration, supragranular layer thickness, and the number of pyramidal neurons. According to the Simmons study, Negro brains tend to be long and narrow (i.e., dolichocephalic with a cranial index approximating 75)—between 3.2 percent and 3.5 percent longer and between 3.5 percent and 4.3 percent narrower on the average than Caucasian brains. Among Europeans, both Mediterranean and Scandinavian stock also tend to be dolichocephalic, and among Africans both the so-called Forest Negroes and Bushmen have been found to display a tendency toward mesocephaly, but in general there seems to be a small but statistically significant difference in the ratios between the horizontal dimensions of black and white skulls. On the other hand, the vertical measurement of Negro brains was found to be much lower than for white brains on the average, and to such an extent that Todd (1923) proposed that this particular deficiency primarily accounts for overall differences in brain size. According to Connolly, Caucasian brains also tend to possess greater fissuration than Negro brains in the frontal and occipital regions, and, of course, the depth of fissuration has long been associated with superior intelligence. Apparently confirming these findings, studies by F. W. Vint in 1932 and 1934 demonstrated that the supra-granular layer of African brains is 16 percent less than in the European brain, a contrast significantly greater than overall brain size differences, for which he found the black average to be 10.6 percent smaller than the European average. This 50 percent increase in supra-granular development as compared to relative brain sizes seems especially significant, Vint claimed, because this region of the brain has been the last to have evolved both phylogenetically and ontogenetically. In our evolution as a species we have acquired this layer at our final stage of advancement over the last couple of hundred thousand years. Likewise, in our early maturation as individuals much of the growth in this layer is postponed to take place after birth in order to permit our head sizes to expand well beyond the limits imposed by our mothers' pelvises. According to Vint, whites seem to advance more than blacks at this post-natal stage of development when the brain enlarges to the size needed to accommodate our mature intelligence.

A post-natal difference in the growth of the cortex and frontal lobes among infants and young children might also explain the peculiar difference between the two races as their brains grow to approximately four times their size at birth by the age of six, when brain size differences become stabilized. At the very earliest stages of growth, it seems, the acquisition of motor skills among black infants exceeds that among white infants to such an extent that they possess perhaps as much as a 20-point to 25-point advantage in average I.Q. if and to the extent that I.Q. can be measured by motor skills at this stage of development. However, white children gradually catch up and then go on to exceed black children in later cognitive development, stabilizing at a 15-point advantage in average I.Q. by their fifth year [ref. *Straight Talk*, (Jensen 1981), pp. 205–6, 211–12]. This precipitous three standard deviation decline for black children from an exaggerated early advantage over white infants of almost two standard deviations to a one standard deviation level of retardation can, of course, be chalked up to environmental deprivation, but it seems to take place among blacks of all social classes, suggesting the problem can more likely be traced to inferior cortical growth subsequent to birth resulting from a different predetermination in genetic coding. Essentially the same pattern occurs when the early developmental advantage of primates (chimpanzees, for example) rapidly declines relative to the continuing advances in cognitive ability to be expected of human development. Just as a swift acquisition of motor skills seems inherited, the later decline in the rate of development for cognitive skills seems equally inherited, and there seems to be a positive correlation between the two. Moreover, the tapering off in black I.Q. seems to occur at exactly the same stage of development, from birth to the age of five, as brain-size enlargement tapers off for blacks as compared with whites, as already discussed in this chapter. Surely these two developmental variations are interconnected.

It should be emphasized here that the apparent similarity between a 15-point deficiency in I.Q. and a 16-percent deficiency in supragranular development is probably accidental, since Vint's measurements were conducted with subjects chosen from malnourished tribes, while the I.Q. differences established by psychometrics are limited to North American blacks who are better nourished and whose intellectual skills probably benefit from a white ancestry that averages between 20 and 25 percent of their genetic makeup. Nevertheless, it seems obvious that statistically meaningful differences in brain size very probably bear a cause-and-effect relationship with differences in I.Q. as established by psychometric experimentation. If, in fact, a .30 correlation exists between I.Q. and brain size, the connection seems inevitable between lower scores in the testing of cognitive skills and inferior development in exactly those regions of the brain that must be exercised in the application of these skills.

It can likewise be speculated that inferior cortical development among Negroes might somewhat diminish the repressive influence of the neo-cortex upon lower brain centers, encouraging such stereotypical black behavior patterns as rhythm, coordination, spontaneity, and a greater susceptibility to emotions resulting from, and directly proportional to, the loss of cognitive skills. It is now generally accepted in the field of brain physiology that the impact of the neo-cortex upon lower brain centers is limited to a complex interplay of inhibitory functions, suggesting that inferior cortical development could, in effect, bear a "liberating" influence for such modes of expression as anger (through hyperactivation of the amygdalae), pleasure-seeking (through hyperactivation of the septal nuclei), superior coordination (through hyper-activation of the cerebellum), and a heightened sense of rhythm (through hyperactivation of the brain stem, the lowest brain center of all). To express anger, for example, the neo-cortex cannot simply trigger the amygdalae; instead, it must repress the function of the hypothalamus in repressing the amygdalae, thus releasing the amygdalae to generate the experience of anger. Suddenly anger occurs through the reduced inhibition of the amygdalae, and the role of the neo-cortex both in containing and then releasing the amygdalae has been strictly repressive. It stands to reason that if the neo-cortex is disproportionately small and plays a less active role, these lower brain centers might be less dominated by its inhibitory influence, leading to somewhat "liberated" behavior patterns. There would continue to be a negative standoff at all levels of neural activity, but the interaction among lower brain centers would be relatively free of cortical input, giving vent to a disproportionate mixture of emotions and spontaneous willfulness at the expense of cognitive restraint. It is to be stressed that absolutely no data has yet been found in support of this supposition, but such a connection seems inevitable if the genetic disadvantage among blacks in prefrontal brain development can be linked with their stereotypical behavior patterns—their quick emotions, their athletic prowess, their taste for rhythm, etc. It seems perfectly reasonable that their losses in one component of brain development might be compensated by gains elsewhere.

What can be asserted with certainty at this point is that careful scientific studies by Ho *et al.* (1980A, 1980B, 1981), Vint (1932 & 1934), Pearl (1934), Todd (1923), Simmons (1942), and Connolly (1950) have established major differences between the races in both the size and proportional development of the brain. These differences probably help to account for the 15-point difference in average I.Q. established by hundreds of psychometric experiments, and they might even help to account for behavioral differences based on disproportionate growth in different regions of the brain. It is unfortunate that all the studies except the three by Ho *et al.* were performed many years ago and therefore lack the sophistication of current research in other fields (for example, psychometrics). Nevertheless, this problem must be blamed on the current avoidance of comparative brain weight data rather than the discovery of any new evidence which supersedes and thus nullifies earlier findings.

If, on the other hand, there were any positive data whatsoever to establish the equality of the races in brain size, we can be assured that neo-Lysenkoists would eagerly parade this data as proof that similarities in intelligence are fully attainable once environmental differences have been eliminated. Numerous supportive studies would be generously subsidized by foundations and government agencies to confirm, and reconfirm, the biological evidence which proves the potential equality of blacks thwarted by prejudice and social injustice. Unfortunately, science tells us otherwise. However, because significant brain-size differences have been found unfavorable to blacks, this entire area of scientific inquiry has been exiled from respectability, as illustrated by Stephen Jay Gould's misguided popularization, *The Mismeasure of Man* (1981), in which he persistently strives to discredit nineteenth century experimentation without admitting that subsequent improvements in cranial measurement eliminated the deficiencies he attacks. Of the five studies listed by Carothers, Gould limits his discussion to Pearl in two brief sentences devoid of factual content. He praises Pearl's concession that nutrition might be the principal cause of racial differences in brain size, but conveniently ignores his experimental data. Gould makes no reference to Todd, Simmons, nor Connolly, though these, along with Pearl, are specifically praised by Carothers for having conducted the only methodologically significant comparisons yet. Nor does Gould mention the data very carefully gathered and published by Khang-cheng Ho and his associates in 1980, a year before the publication of his own book.

V

AFRICAN ORIGINS

O F COURSE, Neo-Lysenkoists stress the importance of environmental deprivation as the cause of any measurable differences between black and white I.Q. averages, but their emphasis upon environment is restricted to the current experience of minority group individuals in the United States. Totally excluded from consideration are the long-term evolutionary consequences of Africa's unique tropical environment for its native population over tens of centuries. The environmental aspects of schooling, family life, and peer-group orientation among black children in the United States are explored ad nauseam, but not the sub-Sahara environmental conditions far more discouraging to social and genetic improvement than the urban crisis endured by American Negroes today. This myopic emphasis upon "hard" environmental data at the expense of longitudinal analysis integrating biology and social adjustment was first put on a systematic footing by the anthropologist Franz Boas, one of the primary instigators of our present tradition in egalitarian research. Its most basic assumption was succinctly explained by his protégée, Margaret Mead, when she declared that the origins of culture pose a question upon which "there is not and cannot be any valid evidence." No tangible data, no origins—it is as simple as that. An exaggerated commitment to hands-on empirical responsibility has thus served to discourage evolutionary comparisons suggesting that at least a few cultures (for example, the Ovaheraro of Africa, who have found no need to invent words representing numbers higher than three) might be more primitive than others, or that their relative lack of advancement might be traceable to genetic deficiency, the product of sustained environmental deprivation. But why not? Why must environmental influences be accepted on a strictly contemporary basis, but not as a longitudinal source of racial differentiation, both social and genetic, over tens of thousands of years?

In fact, a "genetic drift" of as many as 46,000 years has been estimated to separate the Caucasoid and Negroid races, according to Jensen in *Straight Talk* (1981). For the Homo sapiens evolution of 400,000 years, this period represents not more than a ninth of the process of change, but it seems to have produced significant physical differences, some of which are indicated in the previous chapter. Apparently the division between the black and white races began 2,000 generations ago, halfway through the most recent ice age (the so-called Würm glaciation), when sub-Sahara Africa came to be divided from the land mass of Euro-Asia by the simultaneous expansion of the Sahara desert and the Mediterranean sea. Both these natural barriers were produced by deglaciation, and there is ample genetic evidence that they effectively isolated Africans from the nomadic interaction which continued to take place among tribes and clans north of Sahara. The Negro race was restricted to a subcontinent of its own, where its evolutionary advancement seems to have been relatively curtailed, if not reversed, through its continuing exposure to an environment of severe tropical conditions. Indeed, it seems entirely reasonable to speculate that radical differences in the environments north and south of the Sahara-Mediterranean natural barrier were sufficient to have produced separate lines of evolutionary advancement that were comparatively unfavorable to blacks. What else can be expected from almost fifty millenniums of exposure to disease, parasites, predators, and excesses in heat and humidity unknown at higher latitudes? Surely such an existence must have led to genetic consequences more important than skin coloration in differentiating Africa's population from the races which lived north of the Sahara. The harmful influence of tropical climate upon intelligence was persuasively suggested early in our century by Ellsworth Huntington in *Civilization and Climate* (1924) and *The Character of Races* (1925) and his thesis remains credible whether or not it can be absolutely confirmed by contemporary anthropological data.

North of the Sahara-Mediterranean natural barrier, Huntington argued, the faculty of intelligence bestowed a clear-cut evolutionary advantage in coping with seasonal variations and the greater mobility that was possible among tribes in both trade and warfare. Moreover, when hunting and gathering were abandoned in favor of an agricultural economy which established the basis for civilization as we know it today, this major transition was accompanied by a population explosion that necessarily increased the evolutionary advantage of intelligence in particular individuals. The ability to learn fast and to take advantage of new opportunities became the *sine qua non* for survival in a complex and variable social order. Whether in war or peace, those who possessed any superiority in these skills were more likely to prosper, thus raising families of children and grandchildren with roughly the same advantage. The process of winnowing was slow but inexorable, and its ultimate consequence has been the pool of intellectual skills taken for granted today, whose average has been arbitrarily designated as a 100 I.Q.

In the tropical regions of Africa, on the other hand, intelligence seems to have earned a much smaller payoff, so there was arrested development. No benefits came from the ability to predict, to plan and organize, or to come up with an accurate understanding of cause-and-effect relationships except at the most primitive levels. Seasonal change posed no particular problems to be solved, agriculture could only be pursued on a limited basis, the jungle environment discouraged complex tribal interaction, and the population size remained relatively low because of tropical diseases. Most Africans lived in lowland regions which afforded them better protection from hostile tribes as well as greater access to food and water. But they were torpid from unbearably hot and muggy weather and suffered from a multitude of debilitating parasites listed by Carothers to have included hookworm, amebiasis, schistosoma, filaria, Leishmania, and onchocerca, most of which took their toll regardless of the ingenuity of the native population. According to Carothers, Africans were also victimized by such diseases as malaria, dysentery, typhoid fever, smallpox, sleeping sickness, lockjaw, and sickle cell anemia as a genetic byproduct of the body's defenses against malaria. Tropical Africa could be bountiful in providing a family with its full sustenance within a few hundred yards of its domicile, but then again it could just as quickly and arbitrarily bring early death despite their best and most ingenious efforts to protect themselves. For the most part there was little need to think, since the ability to generalize and discern exceptions conferred no particular advantage. Essentially redundant were the virtues of cleverness, resourcefulness, and the capacity to make complex plans and then carry them out. Relatively speaking, I.Q. could take a vacation from the evolutionary struggle, since it did not have much of a role to play. As a result, there was genetic drift in other directions.

VI

PRIMITIVE SOCIETY IN AFRICA

Because of the absence of any written language among African tribes previous to white colonization in the nineteenth century, there is no documentation to give us a clear idea of trends and patterns of change in early African history. As a result, official Negro history in its current formulation has been able to boast of a "golden age" prior to enslavement and colonization by white outsiders. Once upon a time there was bliss and universal harmony in Africa, the story goes, and it was only through the greed and violence of presumably civilized nations that this prelapsarian Utopia was destroyed. However, evidence suggests to the contrary that the European influence was benign compared to the extremes in violence and primitive custom encountered by explorers when they first penetrated Africa's jungles in the early nineteenth century. The brutality of American and European slave traders cannot be denied, nor the genocidal excesses of most European nations when they first subjugated Africa in the late nineteenth century. This applies not only to the Belgian conquest of the Congo River basin, but also to British, French, Portuguese, and German conquests throughout the rest of Africa. However, it is equally true that the African savagery they encountered was much more primitive than generally recognized today. For example, slavery was taken for granted throughout Africa independent of the slave markets abroad, and in fact it was already flourishing when Portuguese shippers first bought into it in the fifteenth century. There was no money in Africa, so slaves seem to have been used as an intertribal currency whose guaranteed exchange value enriched those warlike tribes able to capture slaves on a continuing basis. The dependence upon this source of wealth undoubtedly increased because of Euro-American demand, but its inception must be traced back to earlier centuries, possibly to the influence of Arab slave traders. Moreover, white slave traders seldom captured their prey, but bought them at slave-trading towns from tribes which had dominated the slave market well before whites were included among their customers. We can only deplore the high fatality rate among slaves brought to the New World, but it turns out that the fatality rate was even higher among some of the African river tribes that kept slaves for the purposes of cannibalism. At least one of these tribes, the so-called Fang, depended on cannibalism to such an extent that it supplemented its captured slaves by purchasing slaves from other tribes for the same culinary purpose. Cannibalism was not as universally practiced in Africa as slavery, but a large minority of tribes did resort to it, especially along the Congo river basin. In his fascinating history, *The River Congo* (1977), Peter Forbath summarizes explorers' accounts of their encounters with cannibal tribes, which commonly submerged their victims chin-deep in streams before cooking them, "since suffering was believed to tenderize the meat for the cooking." (Forbath, p. 368).

Social oppression within tribes was likewise much worse than generally recognized today. Polygamy was universal, and wives and children could be killed at the husband's discretion, as documented in Achebe's first novel, *Things Fall Apart* (1959), which tells of his own grandfather's hatcheting to death his adopted son at the demand of a tribal council simply to demonstrate his respect for a local witch doctor. Such sacrifice seems to have been commonplace. Moreover, anybody could be killed or subjected to slavery at the command of a king or emperor, and this power was often abused to an extraordinary degree, as illustrated by H. F. Fynn's (1950) account of the notorious Zulu king Chaka (Baker, pp. 389–90):

> On the first day of Fynn's arrival at court, ten men were carried off to death, and he soon learnt that executions occurred daily. On one occasion Fynn witnessed the dispatch of sixty boys under the age of twelve years before Chaka had breakfasted. . . . On one occasion between four and five hundred women were massacred because they were believed to have knowledge of witchcraft. . . . One of Chaka's concubines was executed for taking a pinch of snuff from his snuff-box. A group of cowherd boys was put to death for having sucked the nipples of cattle. It was the rule in Zululand that no one might eat from any crop until the king had partaken of the first-fruits of the year at a special ceremony. If anyone transgressed, every member of his kraal was executed. At the ceremony the king was accustomed to have many people executed for no other reason than to show his power and cause him to be feared.

Apparently the excesses of Chaka's murderous cruelty were brought to their pinnacle upon the death of his mother, Nandi:

> Universal mourning was immediately ordered. The chiefs and people began to assemble in a crowd estimated at eight thousand. . . . Those who could not force tears from their eyes—those who were found near the river panting for water—were beaten to death by others who were mad with excitement. Toward the afternoon I calculated that not fewer than 7,000 people had fallen in this frightful indiscriminate massacre. . . . Whilst the masses were thus employing themselves, Shaka and his chiefs, the latter surrounding him, were tumbling and throwing themselves about, each trying to excel in their demonstrations of grief by alternate fits of howling. . . . On his first appearance after the massacre Chaka ordered the execution of one of his aunts, who had been unfriendly to Nandi, and of all her attendants (some twelve or fourteen girls). Parties were sent out to execute those who had not come to express sorrow. During a period of one year after Nandi's death, all women found to be pregnant were executed with their husbands.

Where in Asian or European history can one find comparable examples of random brutality? Who among all the rulers of Asia and Europe (Hitler and Genghis Khan included) ordered the execution of sixty children to whet his appetite for breakfast? Or encouraged the murder of seven thousand subjects to express his grief for his deceased mother, then ordered the deaths of all the pregnant women in his kingdom plus their husbands for one whole year after his mother's funeral simply to commemorate her death? I am familiar with arguments that Chaka posed an exceptional case and that the rest of Africa should not be judged by his excesses, but in fact nineteenth century explorers came across several other native kings almost as brutal (for example, Kamurasi, king of Inyoro, and Mutesa, king of Buganda), and it seems naive to believe that such monstrous practices suddenly began when Europeans arrived to record them. There is ample evidence of organized savagery throughout Africa that was only terminated through the stern colonial administration of European nations which resorted to comparable brutality in order to establish their colonial authority. Once they gained this dominance, however, there followed a half-century interregnum of peace and social development probably unmatched in African history. Tribal warfare was eliminated, slavery and cannibalism were minimized, roads were built, children were inoculated, education was systematized, and a relatively consistent body of laws was enforced through the coordination of tribal and colonial authority. Of course, colonial policies were generally prejudicial at the expense of the native population, but at least this population could enjoy the benefits of a systematic rule of government which proscribed the excesses listed above.

It is to be conceded that violence and brutality bear no obvious connection with cognitive deprivation, as demonstrated by countless examples of needless cruelty throughout the modern history of all supposedly civilized nations. Nevertheless, in the case of African tribes, the progenitors of American Negroes, there is a paucity of evidence suggesting any cultural advantages to offset this barbarism. Only the most primitive skills were cultivated in Africa, and most of its tribes seem to have been almost totally incapable of benefiting from cultural diffusion as practiced throughout the rest of the world. Of course, certain basic innovations gained general acceptance, as would be illustrated by the universal custom of slavery, but repeated exposure to a large variety of innovations went unheeded among most African tribes, apparently because they could not rise to the intellectual challenge posed by these innovations. According to Baker in *Race* (1974), coastal tribes were engaged in trade with European and Oriental ships as early as the thirteenth century because of Africa's abundant gold supply (rock-sized nuggets could actually be picked up off the ground). Yet there seems to have been no effort by these tribes to imitate any but the most obviously useful activities. More often than not, cultural diffusion did not occur. From the Berbers the native population did learn the skill of forging iron for weapons, but then they could only perfect this skill without making any new innovations of their own. From European traders they also acquired guinea hens as a source of food, but these were originally an African wild fowl acquired and domesticated by the Egyptians, then transported to Europe, and finally by Europeans back to Africa, their original habitat. Also from European traders Africans acquired tobacco, which became a universal crop within not more than a decade or two when introduced in the early nineteenth century. The speed with which the tobacco plant spread across Africa probably set the record for cultural diffusion among its tribes.

But against this modest record must be compared the total failure of cultural diffusion for more basic innovations such as the simple wheel, which was finally introduced to central African tribes in the late nineteenth century. When David Livingstone brought a wagon into the town of Linyanti, over six thousand local inhabitants gathered to observe its wheels miraculously rotate on their axles, the first time they had seen such an event in their lives. But unlike American Indians, the Africans were undoubtedly exposed to the wheel in earlier centuries, and they did nothing about it. Surely earlier Asian and European traders had brought with them on their ships devices which exemplified the wheel in action, such as the crank, the cannon mounting, and the ship's steering wheel, but apparently these were ignored by coastal tribes. For there is absolutely no evidence in early African history of the wheel in action—of vehicles supported by wheels, of potters' wheels, or of any kind of gear action. The closest any tribe came to the discovery of the wheel was the custom of the Mpongwe tribe to use logs as rollers in moving their large canoes to launching sites (Baker, p. 373). In fact, there is no evidence of any mechanical contrivances devised in central Africa for one part to move against another—for example, in the case of scissors or hinges—and, for that matter, according to one of Baker's nineteenth century sources, ". . .no people of central Africa seems to have acquired the art of joining one piece of wood to another." (Baker, p. 371). Also missing were such fundamental achievements as written language, two-story frame construction, the circulation of money, the use of oxen, horses, and other such beasts of burden, and the establishment of a fixed system of laws to curtail the arbitrary whim of shamans, chieftains, and family patriarchs. Most of the benefits of civilization taken for granted through most of the rest of the world were totally unknown to Africans until European colonization began in the late nineteenth century. Coastal tribes were exposed to these innovations, but the dynamics of cultural diffusion usually taken for granted simply did not catch hold. Of the many possible explanations for this failure, that of a pervasive cognitive deficiency cannot be disregarded.

VII

MODERN AFRICA

FOR THE MOST PART, the level of civilization attained by the ancient Sumerians and Babylonians between two and three thousand, B.C., was more advanced than that of central Africa in the mid-nineteenth century, so it seems in retrospect to have been extraordinarily ambitious on the part of both European colonists and African tribespeople to have tried to bridge the gap with modern civilization in the brief duration of a single century. Cities were carved out of the jungle, roads built, schools and hospitals established, communication lines installed, and, most important of all, the entire population was confronted with the task of converting from tribal to national consciousness. However, once it was free of European rule in the early 1960's, African society has once again lapsed into primitivism despite continued assistance from abroad. In fact, current trends in many African cities suggest a self-destructive mix of the worst features from both levels of cultural deficiency, anachronistic tribal custom augmented by violence, corruption, mob consciousness, and third-world urban cynicism. Attracted to the benefits of modern civilization, Africans seem to have recoiled from its concomitant rules and guidelines, its laws, taxes, and guaranteed social contract. The most glaring example of this retrogressive development is to be found in Uganda, just several decades ago the "Eden" of Africa in its wealth and abundance, but now, after the governments of Obote, Amin, and Obote once again, a land of poverty and despair. Almost as dramatic have been Mobutu's disastrous policies in Zaire, as documented by V. S. Naipaul in his article, "A New King for the Congo: Mobutu and the Nihilism of Africa," included in his book, *The Return of Eva Peron* (1980), as well as in his important novel based on this article, *A Bend in the River* (1979). Naipaul incorporated into his novel the information and personal experience he was able to accumulate during his prolonged visit with a relative in Kisangani (formerly Stanleyville). Many of the details recounted by Naipaul seem exaggerated, but in fact he tones down his story according to independent reports from others who have visited and lived in Zaire. It seems that well over a million individuals have been slaughtered since Zaire was given its independence in 1960, and that its collective standard of living has very quickly plummeted to jungle survival once again. Corruption, extortion, and casual acts of homicide have come to be taken for granted, and even isolated instances of cannibalism have been known to occur. From a personal source I have heard of a young woman who was seen picking over a fresh heap of corpses, carefully making the necessary cuts to remove the liver and kidneys to be eaten in a ritual ceremony later on.

Today, the crisis in Africa seems the most newsworthy

in Somalia, the Sudan, Angola, and Liberia, but one can only guess when and where social collapse will next be grabbing its share of headlines from elsewhere in Africa. The problem has been ubiquitous. Widespread primitivism was documented in *North of South* (1980) in which Shiva Naipaul, V. S. Naipaul's younger brother, recounted his trip through Kenya, Tanzania, Mozambique, and Zambia with embarrassing specificity. More dependent upon the public record, David Lamb told virtually the same story for all of Africa in his book, *The Africans* (1982). Others who have lived and worked in Africa continue to tell the same story. Often they obligingly voice the pious optimism liberals want to hear, but then go on to express their pessimism once sympathetically plied with informed questions. Among those I have met who lived in Africa (one of them a reporter for a weekly national news magazine, who complains of almost total censorship by his editors), it seems to be the consensus that the entire sub-Sahara region is declining into chronic and probably irretrievable primitivism characterized by brutality, corruption, an extreme vulnerability to contagious diseases such as AIDS, and astonishing incompetence in almost every walk of life. Who can forget Samuel Doe of Liberia, who cannibalized one of his political rivals, or Emperor Bokassa of the Central African Republic, who went into a fit of rage and smashed in the brains of several dozen children with his gold-knobbed scepter because they refused to buy their school uniforms from his uniform factory? Less publicized but no less repulsive was the 1980 rioting in Kano, Nigeria, in which from five to seven thousand townspeople were killed because of the widespread belief that members of a fanatic sect were murdering victims to cut out their eyes and mount them in amulets in order to make themselves invisible. This major riot was ignored by the western press until it was offhandedly mentioned by Flora Lewis in a *New York Times* column on May 4, 1981—as yet the only discussion of this incident I have encountered. In her November 9, 1984, editorial upon Ethiopia's famine conditions, Flora Lewis reported the following government response:

> Ethiopia has been charging an import tax of $12.50 a ton for gift food, plus handling and trucking charges of $165 a ton, which go to state-run dockers and transport organizations. One international religious relief group, unable to pay these costs on top of buying the food and getting it to Ethiopia, asked the government if it could bring its own trucks to distribute the gifts. After some hesitation the answer was yes, on condition that all the vehicles be Mercedeses and be turned over to the government free after two years.
>
> Army units patrol the roads to keep the hungry out of the cities. They pick up the spindly legged, swollen bellied people who have been marching for days in search of food, carry them out to the middle of nowhere, and dump them. Children have taken to lying in the road to prevent the units moving on. The patrols have learned to throw scraps of food on the roadside, so the children will scramble for it and get out of the way.

For each and every sub-Sahara nation similar "buried" reports can be dredged up, and though military rule has become commonplace throughout the region in order to maintain at least a rudimentary system of laws (only a couple of the twenty-three democracies first established two decades ago remain under civilian authority), there seems to be no solution to the problem in the foreseeable future. In fact, authoritarian central governments have revived tribal rivalries, even further increasing the likelihood of bloodshed and insurrection.

Of course, a variety of explanations can be found to justify and rationalize this retrogressive trend in Africa, but once again the problem is very likely rooted in the ignorance and irresponsibility of the African mind. Europeans able to observe native Africans in action on a daily basis have almost universally emphasized these qualities, and though their reports may be characterized as being dominated by racial stereotypes, the question remains to what extent these stereotypes have been based on common observation. Three authors featured by Carothers (1972, pp. 93–95) may be quoted to illustrate this consensus, beginning with C. D. Williams' description of the Gold Coast African in 1938:

> Compared with the white races he seems to lack initiative and constructive ideas, although he may be a shrewd judge of the attainments of others. He has a childlike gift for distinguishing the sincere from the false, the shepherd from the hireling. He is almost invariably dishonest. He wishes to attain wealth without expending too much energy. He does not consider there is any obligation to honesty beyond the members of his own family. For them he will give up anything he has and steal anything he has not. Outsiders are fair game and are treated with the utmost callousness. He is conventional and loves talking. He will invent all manner of fabricated excuses out of politeness combined with a facile verbosity. Power of observation is astonishingly defective. . . . They seem to be incapable of sustained effort. . . . An African has little imagination and little humility. His self-esteem is often ludicrous.

Williams went on to praise Gold Coast Africans for their good nature, their cheerfulness, their astuteness, and their uncomplaining fidelity, but he felt their education should emphasize the cultivation of observation, imagination, and judgment; i.e., those skills only indirectly linked with intelligence. A year later, in 1939, D. Westermann emphasized an inability to make long range plans as the primary deficiency shared by all Africans:

> With the Negro emotional, momentary and explosive thinking predominates. . . . dependence on excitement, on external influences and stimuli, is a characteristic sign of primitive mentality. Primitive man's energy is unstable and spasmodic. He is easily fired with enthusiasm for an undertaking and begins his work with great zest; but his interest dies down quickly and the work is abandoned. . . . Where the stimulus of emotion is lacking the Negro shows little spontaneity and is passive. He waits for what is coming to him and evades what is inconvenient or adapts himself to it, instead of bravely confronting the obstacles of life and mastering them. . . . The Negro has but few gifts for work which aims at a distant goal and requires tenacity, independence, and foresight.

Finally, the 1951 report of two French neuropsychiatrists, P. Gallais and L. Planques, seems equally applicable, though they restricted their description to the black population of the French possessions in Central and West Africa:

> The best known traits of the normal psychology of the African are, above all, the importance of physical needs (nutrition, sexuality); and a liveliness of the emotions which is counter-balanced by their poor duration. Sensations and

movements comprise the chief part of his existence. Intellectual life, evocation of the past, and projects for the future preoccupy him but little. Separated from these regulating influences, he lives essentially in the present (in this sense like a child), and his conduct submits to influences and impulses of the passing moment and thus appear "explosive and chaotic."

Obviously, all of these authors may be challenged for their stereotypes, but in fact their observations very effectively reinforce each other in describing a genuine real-life personality profile characterized by a short attention span, an impatience with abstractions, and a relative inability to empathize with others. Once again the basic problem seems to be one of cognitive deficiency, and though its incidence seems to have been greater in some tribes than in others, its pervasiveness in the sub-Sahara region has been taken for granted by most first-hand observers. Here and there black Africans have been found who break the mold, but there are no reports of whole villages or tribes that have fully escaped the deficiencies listed above.

VIII

BLACK POVERTY

EVEN GREATER than the .30 correlation between I.Q. and brain size (see Chapter IV) is the correlation between I.Q. and socioeconomic status (or SES), which has even been found to exceed .50. It seems the higher one's I.Q., the more likely he or she enjoys a better standard of living; vice versa, a lower standard of living suggests the fair-to-middling possibility of a lower I.Q. Of course, there are many exceptions to this rule (especially among academicians), but on balance it seems to be borne out by empirical evidence. There has been a vigorous campaign to challenge this connection by treating I.Q. as a better measurement of social status than of cognitive skills. The 1951 monograph, *Intelligence and Cultural Differences*, by Kenneth Eells, initiated this campaign, incidentally establishing a .20 to .43 correlation between I.Q. and SES for his samplings of white students in the Chicago area. However, Eell's methodology has been seriously questioned (Jensen's *Bias in Mental Testing*, 1980, pp. 520–24), and its difficulties seem to have persisted in subsequent studies along the same lines. More impressive is L. C. D. Kemp's 1955 study, "Environmental and other characteristics determining attainments in primary schools," in which a .52 correlation between I.Q. and SES is proposed tied in with a .73 intercorrelation between I.Q. and scholastic achievement and a .56 intercorrelation between SES and scholastic achievement (Jensen, 1980, pp. 334–36). It is also to be emphasized that Eells and his associates fully acknowledge a strong positive correlation between I.Q. and SES but try to reverse the cause-and-effect relationship, making SES the cause of I.Q. rather than its effect. However, as indicated in Chapter I, recent twins studies (most notably by Osborne, 1980) establish a two-to-one ratio favorable to genetics over the environment. The two obviously interpenetrate in their influence upon I.Q., but the dominance of genetics seems confirmed at this point.

This linkage between I.Q. and SES seems entirely relevant, then, in finding a cause for the pervasiveness of black poverty throughout the world. A lower standard of living among blacks is not just an American problem, but may be found across the globe from Watts to Zanzibar. For in no country, nor in any recorded epoch of history, has the overwhelmingly majority of the black population ever known anything except hand-to-mouth survival at a subsistence level. In societies dominated by a black majority, such as in Africa and the Caribbean Islands, it is the black majority which is impoverished. In societies with large black minorities, such as Brazil and the United States, it is the large black minority which is impoverished. And in societies with small black minorities such as Britain and other American and western European nations, it is the small black minority which is impoverished. No matter what percentage of the total population blacks comprise, no matter what climate they live in, and no matter when they arrived, their economic prospects seem bleak except for a narrow spectrum of middle and upper-middle class families most of whom come from an obviously mulatto background. Amazingly, the very highest levels of affluence ever achieved for the average Negro are to be found here in the United States, where such amenities are taken for granted as glass windows, flush toilets, electrical appliances, telephones, television, automobiles, and mandatory public education through the high school level. Few of these benefits of civilization may be enjoyed by blacks in Africa, South America, and the Caribbean. Even more surprising, black living conditions in the Republic of South Africa are superior to those anywhere else in sub-Sahara Africa. Granted, there has been extreme political oppression of blacks and the colored minorities in South Africa, but this is matched and even exceeded by the arbitrary violence of the military dictatorships elsewhere in Africa. Meanwhile, the standard of living among blacks in South Africa—their housing, schooling and transportation—continues to be the highest in Africa, and as yet there is no appreciable exodus of black South African refugees to bordering nations, as has resulted from political turmoil elsewhere in Africa.

On the other hand, Haiti, the world's oldest nation with continuous black sovereignty, is also one of the world's most pitiful basket cases. Since its bloody emancipation from France in 1801–4, Haiti's living conditions have plummeted to rock bottom with absolutely no prospect of recovery. Here is an island paradise relatively free of Euro-American imperialism for almost two centuries now, but its starving and disease-infested population has been reduced to such an extreme that boatloads of refugees are voyaging hundreds of miles though hazardous seas so they, too, might enjoy the comparative affluence of the American Negro in the state of Florida. Just to live on welfare in the United States seems to offer amenities otherwise exceeding the most optimistic expectations of the average Haitian. Ironically, the same liberals who deplore the treatment of American Negroes on welfare just as strenuously deplore the successful effort of our Coast Guard to prevent Haitians from immigrating to receive the same treatment. Haiti's sovereign responsibility is completely forgotten in face of the obvious extremes in poverty to which its people have been reduced, in large part, through the corruption and ineptitude of their government. Granted, the United States has indeed intervened too much in Haiti, but the cause-and-effect relationship should not be confused. Haitian poverty has been more an inducement to intervention than its effect.

As so effectively documented by Jared Taylor (1992) black poverty seems to be blamed on anybody that can be found except the blacks themselves. The logic might seem valid if a white majority can be held responsible, but white minorities are also blamed, as are white imperialism from abroad and white neglect once its colonists have departed (or been exterminated, as in the case of Haiti). However, exactly the opposite conclusion seems more valid—that substantial economic participation by whites and others (most notably Indians in Africa) is of absolutely crucial importance for maintaining economic growth in the black community. In those African nations in which white investment has been curtailed—for example, Uganda and Zimbabwe—there has been a concomitant reduction in the standard of living, and with no genuine prospects for recovery. Virtually the same thing has happened among the East African nations which expelled their Indian shopkeepers, expecting that blacks would step in and replace them in their economic role. Such did not happen. Confiscated shops went out of business, and the general decline to earlier subsistence levels was accelerated by their loss. In independent African nations which have enjoyed windfall profits, such as Nigeria because of its oil industry, these profits have been almost completely drained off through the corruption and profiteering of a tiny minority, leaving the general population, if anything, even more impoverished than before. The effort persists to pin the blame on somebody else, but there is no convincing evidence that black poverty results from capitalism (the so-called socialist nations of Africa are just as poor as everybody else), from racism (U. S. black poverty is exceeded by black poverty in Brazil, where there is supposedly a better integration among the races), or from any other magic formula of environmental deprivation. Sooner or later it must be recognized that the primary responsibility for black poverty should be traced to blacks themselves, in large part resulting from their problem of cognitive deficiency.

For the mistreatment of blacks to occur in its classic Marxist mold, black workers must be exploited by white capitalists to increase their profits. But exactly where in the world anymore, except perhaps in South Africa's diamond mines, may large contingents of black laborers be found whose energies are sapped to augment the profits of others? Not in Detroit, where black auto workers have gone on unemployment insurance and then welfare compensation. Not in Los Angeles, where blacks receive enough welfare income to be able to spurn the substandard wages and living conditions eagerly sought by Mexican immigrants. Not in Africa, nor in Brazil, nor anywhere else in the world. Quite the opposite, blacks now suffer from unemployment on a world-wide scale and have become collectively dependent to an unprecedented degree upon charity and a variety of make-work schemes concocted by others to give them a halfway decent living. So the Marxist theory of exploitation no longer applies, nor does its boiled-down street-wise rhetoric so often heard among black spokesmen in the United States. If anybody is exploiting anybody else, it is the sizeable population of "minority" charity cases, nations as well as individuals, who cling to this empty rhetoric to justify their continuing dependence upon the generosity of others. And, of course, their rhetoric can only become more strident as current technological advances continue to eliminate them from the labor market. No longer exploitable, they cry exploitation, but their problem lies elsewhere—ultimately with the genetic deficiencies they cannot remedy.

IX

THE AMERICAN GHETTO

IT SEEMS OBVIOUS that the United States is gripped in a bimodal society—one part of it consisting of a 12.3 percent black minority, the other part including almost everybody else from WASPS to Indians, Mexicans, Cubans, and Southeast Asian refugees. There are many serious problems yet among these minority groups, but none seems intractable. However, the situation is different with blacks, for whom social gains have been negligible despite the tens of billions of dollars which have been spent to achieve integration. It is primarily for blacks that two generations of equal opportunity laws, government programs, foundation grants, special education projects, and unprecedented information campaigns by the media (even in comic books, sit-com scripts, and lingerie ads) have netted few improvements beyond what stringent law enforcement extracts in reluctant obedience, beyond what current dollars pay for in temporary cooperation. Today, the social and economic disadvantage of blacks seems, if anything, worse than before, and few deny the statistics of poverty and cultural disadvantage which seem unique to the black minority. In fact, these statistics have often been featured by arch-liberal integrationists in order to justify quotas and increased federal programs targeted for blacks. For this purpose, they try to reverse causation by treating performance deficiencies as the result of social deprivation rather than its source. But the statistics they cannot ignore—for example, the 56 percent poverty rate and the 66 percent birth rate of black single mothers (a rate that increases to 80 percent in Harlem), the high death and disease rates, the upwards of 40 percent "real" unemployment rate among work-age men (including those who have given up looking for jobs), the very high dropout rate from high school, and, of course, the astronomical crime rate, which has converted many urban neighborhoods into dangerous underclass battlefields.

There is indeed no issue today in which official mythology more dramatically diverges from popular opinion than in the recognition that our crime rate is mostly a Negro problem, as in fact it is. Approximately 64 percent of Americans arrested for violent crimes consist of blacks who comprise only 12.3 percent of the population. Strictly in terms of percentages, the chance of blacks being convicted for violent crimes is roughly five times as high as for everybody else. Nationwide in 1976, for example, according to Charles Silberman in *Criminal Violence, Criminal Justice* (1978), "more than half those arrested for murder, nearly half those arrested for rape and two-fifths of those arrested for aggravated assault were blacks." (pp. 118–19). Since the rate of unreported and unsolved crimes is actually much higher in black neighborhoods than elsewhere, these conviction statistics are conservative compared to the level of criminal behavior which actually occurs. Contrary to liberal dogma, the police intervene *less* in black neighborhoods than in white neighborhoods relative to the level of criminal behavior that occurs. Too often the police do not respond to calls in black neighborhoods unless human life is endangered. As a result, blacks are arrested and prosecuted much less frequently proportional to the number of crimes they commit, and so even crime statistics fall short of disclosing the full extent of the problem.

As pointed out by Silberman, black and Hispanic minority groups are roughly the same size in New York City, and the median income among Hispanics has actually been lower than among blacks. Yet 63 percent of those arrested in New York for violent crimes in 1970–71 were black, and only 15 percent were Hispanic, less than one quarter as many. Likewise, the comparative rate of penitentiary confinement between blacks and Mexicans has been 4 to 1 in Texas, 5 to 1 in Arizona, and 3.4 to 1 in Utah (with the recidivism rate jumping to 5 to 1). In San Diego, one of the few American cities to have broken down crime statistics based on ethnicity, black averages exceeded those of Mexicans between 1971 and 1973 by 7.8 to 1 in robbery, by 7 to 1 in homicide, by 4.6 to 1 in rape, by 4.2 to 1 in felonious assault, by 3.5 to 1 in burglary, and by only 2.6 to 1 in theft. On balance the more violent the type of crime, the higher the official statistics unfavorable to blacks, since a higher percentage of non-violent crimes goes unreported in black neighborhoods. However, the much higher violent crime rate among blacks than among Hispanics of comparable economic deprivation might also suggest the importance of additional variables, very likely including fewer inhibitions and greater peer approval for violent behavior (a pattern of "anomie" which is usually more compelling than financial need).

To many the connection between low I.Q. and criminal tendencies seems spurious, but in fact this connection has been repeatedly confirmed by statistical data. According to almost a dozen studies reviewed by Jensen in *Bias in Mental Testing* (1980), the I.Q. average of white juvenile delinquents is between 10 and 12 I.Q. points below that of other white teenagers without a criminal record, putting the average I.Q. of all delinquents, both black and white, almost on par with the overall black average I.Q. in the United States. More generally, the highest crime rate among all Americans, regardless of race, occurs among juvenile delinquents and adult criminals who possess I.Q.'s between 70 and 90. The likelihood of criminal behavior tapers off for I.Q.'s below 50 and above 100. This means that almost half the Negro population can be located in this relatively crime-prone range of I.Q.'s, as compared to less than 10 percent among whites, affording a five-to-one percentage ratio unfavorable to blacks, exactly the disbalance already indicated in violent crime statistics. That is to say, five times as many blacks as whites possess I.Q.'s at levels apparently conducive to criminal behavior, and in fact the violent crime rate among blacks is likewise five times as high. There need be no direct connection between these statistics, but the coincidence is striking, to say the least. For Hispanics, the I.Q.-crime ratio would suggest crime rates approximately three-to-one favorable to blacks, but of course the I.Q. test bias against Hispanics suggests that this ratio should be higher, more in line with the four-to-one violent crime ratio already mentioned. But no wonder there is a far greater likelihood of peer support for criminal behavior in the black community if roughly half its population suffers from cognitive deprivation at levels at which larceny and violent behavior are more likely to occur. The logic of the low-I.Q. criminal seems obvious—if you want it, take it; if you feel wronged, lash out; if challenged, prove your masculinity; if you like her, grab her; and as much as possible show your disrespect (or "dis" in current black slang) to those you dislike. These are all reflexes most of us learn to keep under control, but apparently an adequate I.Q. has much to do with our success in restraining our-selves, once again putting many blacks at a disadvantage in our bimodal society.

Of course, middle-class blacks enjoy relative prosper-ity, and, of course, there are integrated neighborhoods in which race relations are entirely cooperative. However, there are also enormous stretches of broken-down neigh-borhoods inhabited by a black underclass with values and standards of conduct entirely their own. In many of the more ravaged of these areas it almost seems as if African squalor has been thrust into the American melting pot with absolutely no prospect of dissolving into the brew. Trouble often erupts with fires, burglaries, and shootings, but there also seems to be a steady stream of minor in-fractions that transpire on a daily basis—the shouting matches, the blaring radios, the litter thrown about at random, and the deliberate blocking of streets and side-walks without taking into account the needs of others. Too many of the youth ride stolen ten-speed bikes and too many carry radios playing monotonously percussive dance rhythms. Too many low-slung cars tool by as slowly as possible with their radios blaring the same per-cussive rap music as loud as possible. There are also too many boisterous conversations among clusters of loiterers using a heavily slurred black dialect that is almost incomprehensible except for its obvious phatic appeal ("Hey, man," etc.) and its pervasive male-assertive expletives such as "motherfucker," "fuck you," and "shit, man." These usually serve as intensifiers meaning, "I really want to emphasize my point," but they also provide breathing space to let dull ideas catch up with the quicker flow of words. Of course, verbs remain unconjugated, pronouns undeclined, and dead metaphors (for example, "wheels" as an obvious synecdoche for the automobile) almost totally inaccessible to variety. Often conversations shift into an exchange of threats and denials spiced by enough exaggerated outgoing laughter to keep relationships friendly, but now and again they degenerate into loud arguments which can be heard more than a block away if sufficiently lubricated by liquor.

A kind of grab-and-discard psychology generally prevails in these ghetto neighborhoods, so anything left outside the house or apartment quickly disappears. Distinctions between larceny and carelessness break down, since the possessions of others have merely been "borrowed," then transferred to others, and nobody can quite remember when and by whom. Maybe they were sold, but the money has already been spent, or lent to somebody else, or used to pay a debt. Who cares? Obviously, widespread unemployment contributes to this carelessness, but so do thrill-seeking, macho status, anti-white resentment, and sheer lack of concern, since everybody without a visible means of support seems able to tap into welfare money either by bearing children or by joining an extended domicile of one or more who do. As many as two dozen children and young adults can occupy a household exclusively supported by welfare motherhood—the ghetto's most successful industry. Whatever is stolen gets fenced for the smallest fraction of its value and then spent on liquor, drugs, gambling debts, gasoline, and trinkets for girlfriends, not on bread, milk, and other such basic necessities already paid for by food stamps. Of course, "need" remains a major consideration, but more fundamental are the spontaneous demands of an anti-social lifestyle that seem more tied in with cognitive deficiency than sociologists are willing to admit. The problem exists—this they concede—but they consider it heresy to suggest a cause-and-effect relationship by which genetics plays at least as important a role as social conditioning.

Does this mean that all blacks are doomed to poverty because of our bimodal crisis in the United States? Not at all. There is a growing black middle class which more or less confirms the overlap that exists between black and white normal distributions in I.Q. According to data gathered by Jensen and others, this middle class may be recruited from the 16 percent of the black population (or 4,798,000 according to the 1990 census) who are more intelligent than 50 percent of the whites, and from the .1 percent of the black population with I.Q.'s exceeding 130, high enough to permit success in almost any field of endeavor. A tenth of one percent might seem a rather small figure, but to divide 29,986,000 blacks by 1000 leaves 29,986, give or take a few thousands, who can fully compete with 130-I.Q. whites in coping with abstractions, indeed with every circumstance of modern life. The existence of such a qualified minority is confirmed in many occupations beyond music, sports, and entertainment—for example, in literature as exemplified by the genuine cultural achievement of such black authors as Richard Wright, Ralph Ellison, James Baldwin, Toni

Morrison, and others. Also to be respected are the political contributions of such figures as Frederic Douglas, W.E.B. Du Bois, Booker T. Washington, A. Philip Randolph, Martin Luther King (his record of plagiarism notwithstanding), Malcolm X, Jesse Jackson, and many others, many of whom have displayed ample intelligence in their pursuit of black liberationist objectives.

However, the lower end of the I.Q. normal curve for our black population cannot be ignored either, and here is where the bimodal crisis seems formidable, if not insurmountable. If everybody with an I.Q. between 68 and 83 is to be classified as "feeble-minded," as once officially decreed, then almost half the black community fits this description at best! Likewise, if a "moron" may be identified as anybody with an I.Q. between 52 and 67, as once officially decreed, this means that roughly 15 percent of our black population fits this description at best—150 times as many black people as in the 130-plus I.Q. category! In other words, three out of every twenty blacks treading our sidewalks may be clinically diagnosed as morons, but only one out of a thousand as having 130-plus I.Q. skills. This lopsided distribution as compared to white probabilities imposes a major burden upon our society, especially in face of the current equal opportunity campaign to implement job and educational quotas based on the false assumption either that I.Q. differences are totally meaningless or that they come from environmental deprivation and can easily be eliminated.

Over the last few years the unrealized potential of black intelligence has been incessantly packaged for public consumption, suggesting the ready accessibility of all blacks to improvement if only given the chance. However, the 50 percent of the black community who fit the dullard category at best (to say nothing of the 15 percent who fit the moron category at best) present an entirely different case. These are the individuals who can barely spell out written messages, who fumble the simplest arithmetic, who get confused by instructions, who keep silent to mask their deficiency, who frequently resort to empty laughter, who throw away their income on junk food and cheap, gaudy possessions, who arrive late at appointments (or not at all), who try to intimidate by glowering, and who resort to violence because they cannot otherwise help themselves. Almost half of our black population can more or less be expected to display these tendencies, and they cannot make a sudden and miraculous transformation into productive and self-sufficient middle-class citizens, no matter how much time, money, and effort are expended in the effort—not if their problem ties in with low I.Q., two-thirds of which is the responsibility of genetics. If this is the case, the only way to help this segment of the black community is to present them with an economic and educational challenge they can cope with, and the first crucial step in this direction is to scale down everybody's expectations to a more realistic level.

X

MY EXPERIENCE WITH BLACK STUDENTS

FOR MY FINAL USE of empirical data suggesting inferior cognitive skills among blacks, I want to refer to our educational crisis today based on my personal experience in teaching for over two decades at the college level. Throughout my career I have dealt with many hundreds of black students, a few of them truly intelligent, some of average ability, but the great majority with very modest talent indeed. Most seemed well motivated but almost hopelessly incompetent in dealing with both Standard English and the task of putting to paper ideas and impressions they wanted to communicate. For a couple of years I helped to train dozens of black paraprofessionals to become public school teachers by encouraging them to memorize questions and answers they were likely to encounter on standardized qualification tests. Most of them succeeded and became certified public school teachers, better than white teachers for their neighborhood schools, I reasoned, because of their excellent rapport with their non-integrated black classes. However, all but two or three of these future teachers remained almost totally illiterate in my opinion. Most failed to grasp even the most rudimentary concepts of language and literature despite their intense commitment to educating themselves. Their prose was dominated by run-on sentence fragments that could be justified neither in standard dialect nor in anything resembling the official black dialect celebrated by William Labov and others. All in all, they seemed totally unprepared to serve as teachers except for students with the same skills deficiencies and with no better chance of rectifying them. Unfortunately, integrationist policies soon shifted, and the abandonment of neighborhood schools resulted in the dispersal of these teachers throughout the entire city school system, all the more effectively spurring the white exodus to private, parochial, and suburban schools.

I have also heard all the scuttlebutt about black colleagues who did not exactly write their own books, and I have sat on Ph.D. dissertation committees for black candidates for whom editorial revisions by department facilitators were probably so extensive that the staff itself better deserved to be given the degrees than the candidates themselves. Throughout my teaching career I have likewise exercised a tacit double standard of grading blacks up a notch for whatever they did—a "D" for "F" work, a "B" for "C+" work, etc., and this grade inflation has obliged comparable, if slightly reduced, grade inflation for white students, too. How could I give one of my black students a "B−" for "C" work, for example, unless I also gave white students "B's" for "B−" work? As a result, all grades have been inflated so blacks could be encouraged without too blatantly cheating the whites. I suspect a large majority of the teaching profession has fallen into the same trap, though few are willing to talk about it.

Among the five black students I tested one semester several years ago, four scored 95 on the Clarke Institute multiple-choice version of the WAIS verbal I.Q. scale, the fifth a healthy 110. By far the least competent of this group was a 30-year-old woman I can call Lucinda, who answered the first two questions as follows on her final examination in my upper division course in advanced composition:

1. Write a sentence containing a comma fault, then a revision of this sentence in which the comma fault is eliminated.

   ANSWER: He was stock, the boy was riding his tricycle
   In riding the tricycle, the stock strick the boy.

2. Explain the "organic" relationship between a term paper's thesis statement and its outline (if necessary extending your explanation onto the back side of the page).

   ANSWER: It tell how the term paper will develop in a more fully explantion.

My final examination also included a single essay question asking each student to summarize his or her semester's term paper which had been turned in the previous week. I also asked how its thesis might be challenged and what could be said in response. None of my students knew this would be the question, but of course they were all sufficiently informed to deal with it if they had researched and written their own term papers. All of them were upper division students taking the course at an advanced level, and they enjoyed the added advantage that they had chosen their own topics for these term papers. Lucinda's answer to this question may be quoted in its entirety, once again without changing any of her errors:

> My basic point in my term paper was that Black mothers and daughters had it rough in life and that no one in society really understood the hard life. They had it,, hard in a "white world" that caused a lot discomfort with Black people in trying to get along today. Blacks are at each other throat not with each other against one another. This also makes that some how that Black people have got to find some way of bringing unity together in the "white world"
>
> White World have not helped the black people to get out of this 'Knot" that blacks are in by low paying jobs, this underminding life that Blacks have.
>
> Black mothers and daughters have been the back bone as well as the Indians of America. To get what America is today because the White people sure did do it because "White" did want to get their hands dirty.
>
> My argument is that Black Women have to come a long way still in order to improve half way free they got to make a strong unity among women not fighting against one another over men, jobs, way of life.

Whatever the merits of Lucinda's thesis, her prose was obviously a hopeless jumble of slogans and resentful stereotypes in which the only discernible thinking came from the way she shifted from one complaint to the next, then back again. She did not try to answer the second and third parts of my question though she completed her exam well before the time limit had been reached. She herself tried to explain her difficulties on the last page of her exam, apparently referring to questions upon usage and punctuation I had announced would be included in the test: "I had sentences memoize for test but when go to class and the test my mind went blank." As if memory alone might have helped her to pass the test, as if the tens of thousands of dollars spent on her special education through her senior year of college would bear anything but the most marginal results.

Why did I give Lucinda a "D" in the course instead of the failing grade her performance deserved? Primarily because she was black, thus deserving the benefit of the doubt in her desperate effort to meet white standards. It is likewise to be remembered that her 95 verbal I.Q. puts her two-thirds of a standard deviation above the average black I.Q. in the United States and fully at the level of most of my earlier paraprofessional students who in fact became secondary school teachers. Compared to other blacks across the nation, she can be located at perhaps the seventy-fifth percentile in her verbal performance, just barely in the top quarter among all American Negroes. Her performance level was below average for most of the black students I have been working with in recent years, but not to an extreme degree, and in fact it was much better than might be expected of the average ghetto resident who stays away from college. Of course, some blacks rise above this deficiency (a colleague in Black Studies, for example, might actually test out as a genius of sorts), but for a great majority of blacks college-level academic demands continue to pose a genuine ordeal. Unfortunately, too many of them try to make up the difference with phony excuses, with taking nothing but "gut" classes by generous teachers, with an inordinate reliance upon a variety of editorial "helpers" provided by black fraternities and college skills centers, and with an unhealthy dose of mock intimidation ("Why yo no gi' me an 'A'?") The average professor is left with the task of coping with the situation as well as possible and not complaining too loudly for fear of being taken as a bigot. He realizes he is up against his own bimodal crisis, but he possesses sufficient academic experience to recognize that discretion is the better part of valor.

XI

THE NEW AMERICAN DILEMMA

NEO-LYSENKOISTS HAVE BEEN REMARKABLY SUCCESS-FUL in convincing the American public that there is abundant scientific evidence in support of their egalitarian bias, but in fact no hard data can be found in psychometrics, craniometrics, physical anthropology, cultural anthropology, archaeology, African history, sociology, or police statistics to justify their claims. Their strategy seems essentially negative. All they can do is aggressively discount the vast accumulation of evidence suggestive of I.Q. differences by evoking the ever-useful environmentalist argument that measurable differences must necessarily be traced to environmental conditions on the *prima facie* assumption that ALL IS OTHERWISE EQUAL in the distribution of talent among the world's population. Confronted with tomes of irrefutable data about I.Q. differences, neo-Lysenkoists reply, "Granted, but don't you see . . .", launching into their predictable litany of environmentalist claims. Confronted with comparative crime and welfare rates or with Africa's extreme primitivism through the end of the nineteenth century and with the total collapse of its democratic institutions today, they once again reply, "Granted, but don't you see . . .", and once again knee-jerk environmentalism lurches into view. Confronted with measurable differences in brain size, they must take a slightly different tack, as they do, by denying the evidence, by denying the relevance of cranial size to I.Q., by challenging the validity of I.Q. scores, and only then by concluding, "After all, environment, don't you see . . .", once again invoking this hallowed shibboleth to sanctify their predictable evasiveness. However, the raw truth remains—they possess absolutely no credible evidence of their own that holds up to empirical verification beyond their environmentalist's faith that the universe itself shares our laudable egalitarian ideals by having created all races exactly equal. This principle of absolute equality might not apply to all individuals, mind you, but certainly, they argue, to the normal-curve distribution for all races. Presumably, there is genetic convergence toward perfect statistical equality which is so powerful that bigger and more fundamental forces of environment—the thrust of almost fifty thousand years' isolation in sub-Sahara Africa's tropical climate—have borne no impact whatsoever on the intellectual capacity of those whose ancestors endured such an existence. This is the paradox we are expected to believe—an environmentalist rejection of environmental impact except as the ongoing daily ordeal among certain dispossessed minorities in the United States today. Environmental stress can only be emphasized with the caveat that it affords a clean slate (or zero-base origin) for each individual at the moment of birth or conception. Let blacks be provided the same social benefits, the argument goes, and within not more than a couple of generations most of them will o'erleap their oppressive legacy to be fully competitive with the rest of us at calculus, on the computer, and in the management of their daily affairs. This we are supposed to believe despite the discouraging evidence that little of the sort has happened yet either in the United States or anywhere else—despite the testimony of psychometricians, despite the measurements of an inferior pre-frontal brain development, despite a prodigious national investment which seems to have been largely wasted in costly boondoggles over the past thirty years.

A second and perhaps more attractive "liberal" assumption would be that we have no absolute and irrefutable proof yet of black deficiency in intellectual capacity, so it would be more in keeping with our Constitutional and Judaeo-Christian ideals to assume potential equality as the best way to encourage at least a narrowing of social differences among the races. Even if genetic racial equality is only a myth, it can at least be defended as a "useful" myth comparable to all the rest which help to give adhesion to our social fabric. If cultural harmony depends upon the general acceptance of a few benign fictions that mesh truth and the desirable improvements we wish to impose, why not add black equality to the brew as prob- -ably one of our very most important social imperatives in need of this kind of reinforcement? Why embarrass one of our minorities? Why not pretend equal potential in order to produce at least a better and more equitable distribution of our national income? Cannot we give credence to the benign fiction of perfect genetic uniformity just to be able to maximize social justice throughout our nation? When it comes to race relations, it seems as if the capital-"T" truth might for once take a back seat to the democratic values to which we all subscribe.

I can sympathize with this vision, and in fact I have tried to abide by it throughout most of my educational career. However, it strikes me as increasingly obvious that the myth of black equality has become more destructive than other collective illusions, since a rigorous official commitment to its validity has already produced considerable social upheaval and can be expected to accelerate this trend until our entire society is jeopardized. It is one thing to dangle the American dream before the eyes of individuals who are incompetent to achieve it even with the collaborative support of others, but quite another to try to reorganize our society from top to bottom in order to impose this impossible dream, and then, when nothing seems to work, to compound dislocations many times over again in the fruitless effort to remedy previous failures. This strategy seems to have been our national commitment since the mid-sixties, and its fullest consequences are only beginning to be felt. Several more decades of comparable effort, and we might no longer be able to take for granted that luxury called democracy simply through having squandered our collective destiny in pursuit of an unachievable goal. Brainwashed by liberal rhetoric, blacks are increasingly dissatisfied with their circumstances, while whites have learned to combine flight and hypocrisy in their effort to cope with black demands. Our social fabric is visibly declining in our cities, in our schools, and in the behavioral disorientation of our children, and it can only become even further damaged unless our national priorities are put on a more realistic basis.

Most Americans seem willing to give blacks a somewhat bigger piece of the pie, but there is also the understandable concern that current patterns of social deterioration must be stopped. The condition to be observed in our inner cities seems to be inexorably spreading into adjoining neighborhoods, into the suburbs, even into state and national politics. Unless a basically different approach can be found, modest black improvements will continue to be overmatched by white sacrifice and a general sense of malaise and collective impoverishment that we should all be eager to prevent, blacks as well as whites. It is not simply a matter of taking from one to give to the other. More likely, a qualitative floor effect must be avoided at the threshold of inefficiency beneath which everybody loses. If low I.Q. continues to be imposed upon our society by government edict, a certain percentage of our GNP might still be diverted to those victimized by this particular affliction, but more important will be the general loss for all concerned. We will eventually come up with less to divide, and with an even greater sense of injustice among both blacks and whites.

There are four general areas—education, employment, crime, and welfare—in which the myth of black equality has already borne obviously harmful results. Each of these areas deserves a chapter of its own for demonstrating the cost to our society that has resulted from our dedicated commitment to this myth.

XII

OUR PRESENT CRISIS IN EDUCATION

THE INTEGRATION of our educational system is an important initial step in bringing about the effective integration of our society based upon individual talent rather than quotas or prejudicial stereotypes. Consequently, our nation's efforts in this direction since the Supreme Court's 1954 Brown decision seem on the whole justified. However, there have been chronic and apparently insoluble difficulties in the ongoing effort to expose blacks with inferior cognitive skills to educational materials they simply cannot comprehend. On the assumption that these blacks might profit from an education fully as demanding as that which is provided to the majority of whites, billions of dollars have been spent to force-feed them with this alien system of knowledge despite their incompetence to learn anything beyond the rudiments of reading, writing, and arithmetic. To guarantee this "equal" opportunity, our nation's educational establishment has resorted to forced busing, the elimination or reduction of ability-level tracking, modular uniformity in the materials taught, test-preparation teaching, the imposition of rigid equal-opportunity guidelines in the hiring of teachers, and huge budget expenditures upon Head Start and a variety of similar catch-up programs stretching from nursery school to the lubricated Ph.D. As a result, our educational system is far more expensive to administer than before, and at the same time the education taught in our schools is sinking to unprecedented levels in the history of our nation. Television plays its role in this decline, as do the programmed learning packages foisted on our schools by a number of publishing houses. But the single most important factor in bringing our educational system to its knees has probably been the indiscriminate mixture of ability levels forced on our students by integrationist guidelines insisted by courts spurred on by the N.A.A.C.P. and other such benevolent organizations. Sometimes school integration has worked because of a solid white majority among students in excess of 60 percent to 70 percent and because of a continued *de facto* segregation through tracking slow students into classes appropriate to their ability levels. However, when the black minority exceeds from 30 percent to 40 percent of the student body, when the tracking of students based on ability levels is abandoned because of its inevitable "racist" consequences, and when the materials taught are absurdly simplified so as to be grasped equally well by both black and white students, entirely different results soon become obvious. As Achebe put it, things fall apart. Like the slow learners among white students, blacks with inferior learning skills can also be expected to slow down the learning process for others and to try to vindicate themselves in adolescent fashion by means of disruption, intimidation, and the aggressive display of their superior street sophistication. The only difference is that the small and controllable minority of whites who buttressed their self-esteem by resorting to this strategy thirty years ago has been supplemented by a large racially isolated sub-population whose learning difficulties seem organically connected with their cultural identity. For too many of these students it becomes almost a matter of honor to fail in school, and in many of our larger cities this pattern of failure is guaranteed by often extraordinary antisocial behavior.

If there were a fixed balance in the mixture of black and white students, and if differences in their learning abilities merely averaged out so that a 33 percent enrollment of black students produces not more than an overall 5 percent or 10 percent loss in educational results, the sacrifice could be absorbed in the interests of improved democracy. Unfortunately, this is not what happens. Instead, what must be endured is a severe breakdown in the educational process as well as chronic misbehavior and the relentless intimidation of serious students, both black and white, on the playground, in the halls, in the restrooms, and even in classrooms. Moreover, the disruption of classes is likely to become a test of the black students' black consciousness and macho self-esteem, all the more rapidly destroying the necessary atmosphere for providing an adequate education. Inevitably the departure of white students accelerates to private, parochial, and suburban schools, and with their departure the rate of decline likewise accelerates until the school (or school district) becomes a burned-out shell as compared to its former role in the community. At this point liberal integrationists perk up with indignation that *de facto* segregation has once again been allowed to crystalize, and so the necessary steps are taken to incorporate the outlying school districts to which most of the white families have fled to avoid the problem. Thus the cycle is renewed on a larger and more inclusive scale: buses are driven farther, children get up earlier in the morning, and with luck the process takes place at a slower tempo.

The problem is far more serious in major cities than politicians and the news media are willing to acknowledge. The cover article of the May 9, 1983, issue of *Newsweek*, for example, was devoted to the issue of school deterioration without once mentioning race—the single most important consideration, as might be guessed by the ample number of black children in the photographs used to illustrate the article. On a more personal level, I can recall when my daughter attended a large integrated metropolitan high school in which her advanced English class was frequently featured on local TV news programs to offer visible evidence of successful integration in the school system. No other classes were televised—just hers alone in which there seemed to be a healthy racial mix. One day, to the amusement of everybody involved, a television crew coming to film another of its mini-episodes of racial harmony was actually forced to step over blood puddles and broken glass from a bottle fight that had just erupted in the hall outside her classroom. Needless to say, there was no mention of the bloody scuffle in the local news program that evening. Instead, the teacher could once again be seen posing a question to a mixed group of attentive students, followed by hands eagerly shooting up from blacks as well as whites (my daughter's included). Even less newsworthy was the episode in which students threw a teacher down a staircase, the way some taller students could jump from desk tops to swing from lights suspended from the ceiling, and the constant harassment my daughter received in another class from a male student seated next to her who wanted her to accept his services as a pimp in the local red light district. My wife and I were grateful when the teacher, once aware of his importunities, shifted his seat to a different part of the classroom.

The official mythology of productive gains having been achieved in racial harmony in our public school system might seem necessary to encourage and help bring about the needed changes in our social fabric, but when this mythology flies in the teeth of anything that can be truly accomplished and reinforces the ignorance of the public regarding our educational crisis, its value as a benevolent public relations strategy becomes dubious at best. A better and more effective integrationist program can only be initiated by acknowledging our current difficulties rooted in a bimodal distribution of academic skills, and by accepting the need to cultivate the full potential of each student based on individual performance levels and without trying to impose (and disguise) rigid integrationist quotas where these quotas simply will not work. Unless this more flexible strategy is adopted by our educational establishment, the exponential deterioration of our urban and suburban schools can be expected to continue.

XIII

OUR PRESENT CRISIS IN THE JOB MARKET

CONSIDERING THE MANY BILLIONS OF DOLLARS spent by the federal government to improve the plight of the American Negro community, it would seem that some kind of statistical evidence might be found to suggest changes for the better. Such evidence was dredged up by Carlos C. Campbell, a former official of the Reagan administration, in his October 30, 1984, *New York Times* editorial, "Distrust Liberal 'Foxes,' " in which he understandably tried to emphasize the positive achievements of the federal government in race relations. His use of statistics may be quoted in its entirety:

The number of blacks enrolled annually in colleges and universities nearly doubled between 1970 and 1980. Since 1960, the number of black doctors has tripled; the number of black lawyers has increased sixfold. In 1965, there were fewer than 300 black elected officials; today there are more than 5,500. The number of black businesses has more than doubled from the 163,000 reported in 1969. Black Enterprise magazine reported on the nation's top 100 black-owned businesses for the first time in 1972; at that time, they had gross sales of $473 million. A decade later the "Black Enterprise 100" had gross sales exceeding $2 billion.

This evidence has indeed been encouraging, and it suggests the emergence of a black middle class—those who have become doctors, lawyers, businessmen, and elected officials—primarily resulting from massive federal assistance. However, relative cognitive deficiency is not to be ruled out compared to whites of equal socioeconomic status, as demonstrated by the better rates of growth among black professionals in fields in which cognitive skills play a smaller role—in politics more than law, in law more than medicine. It also seems relevant that only twenty-four blacks received Ph.D.'s in engineering nationwide in 1979, only thirteen in mathematics, and only four in computer sciences. For fields such as these, in which cognitive demands are exceptionally high, integrationist efforts have been particularly unsuccessful simply through lack of numbers. For other fields with lower demands, the increased participation of blacks seems to result as much from reduced educational standards as from quotas, federal aid, and the elimination of prejudicial barriers.

What has happened since 1980? According to Jared Taylor:

> In 1986 only 820 blacks earned Ph.D.'s in the whole country, and half of these were in education. Not a single black got a Ph.D. in geology, aerospace engineering, astronomy, geometry, astrophysics, or theoretical chemistry. No black got a Ph.D. in European history, Russian, Spanish,

German, architecture, or the classics. American universities gave out 8,000 Ph.D. degrees in physical sciences and engineering, but blacks earned only 39 of them.

In 1987, of the 290 doctorates granted in electrical engineering, not one went to a black. Blacks earned 3 of the 281 doctorates in chemical engineering, 2 of the 240 degrees in mechanical engineering, and 5 of the 698 doctorates in astronomy and physics. (p. 166).

The record continues to be bleak, and if and when the number of black Ph.D.'s increases, the first assumption one must draw is the likelihood that Ph.D. programs have been watered down to meet the extraordinarily high demands for black Ph.D.'s in both colleges and the business world.

The problem seems far more serious for the great majority of blacks who seek average jobs with average skill demands. There is obviously a serious problem of underemployment, so federal job quotas have been imposed at schools, colleges, government agencies, and business corporations dependent upon government contracts and licenses. These quotas were justified by the Supreme Court's Bakke decision of 1978, Weber decision of 1979, and Fullilove decision of 1980, confronting just about every large employer in our country with the same problem—that unless it hires a sufficient number of black employees to demonstrate its adequate commitment to equal opportunity, the federal government is prepared to take punitive action which is guaranteed, if nothing else, to impose prohibitive court costs whether the case is won or lost. This Draconian enforcement policy seems more than adequate in helping to give blacks a fair share of our economy, but black underemployment continues, in part because too many blacks are totally unqualified to be hired, but also in part because too many black employees, once hired, have cost their employers far more in theft, incompetence, and legal fees than they have contributed in their work productivity. As explained to me by the personnel director of a major urban bank, longitudinal studies conducted by his office have established that the participation of black employees actually produces a net loss in profits per black worker as opposed to the average net gain employees are expected to earn for their companies. His bank has tried to hire and put on display enough blacks to keep government lawyers at bay, but in doing so it has saddled itself with an additional financial burden resulting from theft, inefficiency, deteriorating morale, and, most devastating of all, high court costs from trying to settle these other problems when they get out of hand. It seems the federal government provides free legal aid to all black employees dismissed from their jobs regardless of the specific reason for their dismissal. Add and subtract on a double entry basis, and American business today understandably refrains from hiring any more blacks than necessary despite the pressure to appease the federal government.

It has been proposed by Jensen and others that slow workers can perform relatively simple tasks more satisfactorily than others once they have been taught to do so on a more or less habitual basis. There might be some truth to this, but with the caveat that any job requiring extensive human interaction automatically puts a premium on verbal intelligence in even the simplest acts of cooperative endeavor. The 86-I.Q. telephone operator might be able to plug in most of her calls through the day, but at least a few of her callers will need additional information, some of it hard to come by, whereupon her deficiency can only become a problem to everybody concerned. Put enough like her in her office and business can be expected to decline; put enough in all the offices across our nation and once again a floor effect comes into play, this time through inferior national output contributing to a general falling off in our economy as compared to other nations. Inevitably the competitive edge must shift to multinational corporations able to transfer their productive facilities elsewhere, leaving behind an army of unproductive consumers, both black and white, as well as the service industries needed to keep them happy.

XIV

OUR PRESENT CRISIS IN CRIME
PREVENTION

THE CRIME STATISTICS SURVEYED in Chapter VIII disclose the responsibility of black Americans, usually between fourteen and twenty-six years old, for much of the crime wave which has swept the United States over the last two decades. Some liberal apologists have argued that these statistics are misleading because blacks have been prejudicially singled out for punishment, but in fact, as earlier indicated, there is a much greater likelihood for crimes to go unreported in ghetto areas, suggesting a crime rate even higher than indicated by official statistics for minor and non-violent infractions. Meanwhile, it cannot be discounted that 64 percent of Americans arrested for violent crimes consist of blacks, though our black population comprises only 12.3 percent of our population and though there are necessarily more unsolved crimes by blacks in ghetto areas that are omitted from these statistics. The disproportionate role of black criminals is thus too big to be ignored, and it seems amply confirmed by the personal experience of almost everybody who has lived in American cities over the past several decades. In effect, the American criminal justice system simply does not work very well in discouraging the black criminal. Our history of English common law as modified by constitutional principles might serve the great majority of middle-class whites with a 100-I.Q. average, but it seems almost hopelessly ineffective up against the typical low-I.Q. black malefactor who often seems confused whether he is in trouble or not, whether he betrays his trust with others or not, and sometimes whether he wants to kill and rape or not. For most of us the mere existence of a system of justice serves as sufficient deterrence reinforced by our personal codes of ethics. For the low-I.Q. black criminal these constraints prove to be comparatively minor, so our nation's complex system of appeals and due process guidelines merely gives him more leeway to engage in criminal activities. He can depend upon his full constitutional rights—whether he understands them or not—to keep him on the streets able to do his thing up against anybody who gets in his way at the wrong time. He can freely stash stolen goods in his house, confident that nobody will bother to come up with the search warrant needed to permit it to be searched. He can intimidate others from testifying against him. He can brazenly display, sell, or give away stolen possessions, confident that if he is interrogated his right to counsel lets him get away with claiming, for example, that he had just that day (or the night before) bought these stolen possessions from a total stranger. On those rare occasions when he is apprehended and booked for a crime, he can pay his low bail and resume his criminal activities to help pay for his lawyer's fees. He can also plea bargain with the prosecutor, admitting all his earlier crimes in exchange for a reduced sentence for the one with which he is charged. This lets these other crimes be taken off the books, recorded as "solved" crimes though, of course, none of the stolen property has been recovered. If by any chance this "victim" of white justice is sent to prison, he can get out on probation early and disregard parole conditions by resuming his criminal career elsewhere, if necessary in another state. He is almost totally free to do as he pleases, protected from effective retribution by the very criminal justice system which had once been set up to discourage his kind of behavior. There is no cleverness on his part—he simply does what he does, and the criminal justice system takes care of the rest. And because he can get away with it, his friends join in, and their friends too, until the police are forced to write off crime control except in the most severe cases or when public relations becomes an urgent matter of concern.

As to be expected, the United States endures the very worst crime rate among industrial nations and at the same time offers the world's most generous guarantees for protecting the rights of suspected criminals. But the principal explanation for this debacle in law enforcement mostly lies in the contradiction that we are trying to apply unduly civilized standards in the effort to curtail criminal behavior, much of which is the product of severe cognitive deficiency. We want to maintain our constitutional rights despite our multi-racial composition which puts us in a class with the nations of Africa and South and Central America, all of which have found it necessary to resort to far more stringent law enforcement policies. Typically in the third world, a small army of underpaid policemen dressed as soldiers occupies all potentially troublesome street corners of the cities, ready and able to call in reinforcements from nearby street corners when necessary. If a crime is committed, these policemen converge from every direction, take all necessary steps to apprehend the suspects, and then haul everybody to a police station where aggressive interrogation techniques might be used before any lawyers are permitted to enter. The system is arbitrary and often brutal, but it actually encourages the public to assist in apprehending criminals, confident that these criminals are primarily in jeopardy, not themselves. Granted, we do not want to resort to such a system of justice in order to turn the tide against criminal misbehavior here in the United States. Our constitutional freedoms do seem worthy of perpetuation, and we do want to live under a system of government which guarantees these freedoms. However, it also seems obvious that some kind of compromise is necessary to bring our high crime rate under control. We need to streamline our legal system and restore some of its efficiency which seems to have been lost as a result of the flood of Supreme Court rulings since the mid-sixties. To convince the typical 70–85-I.Q. malefactor (white as well as black) that he should avoid rape, theft, armed robbery, and the like, we need to improve the likelihood of a swift and visible punishment that fixes in his mind the inexorable connection between crime and its painful consequences. Since he thinks in a relatively simple fashion, the penalty for his anti-social behavior must be dramatized to him with comparable simplicity, and his punishment must obviously exceed his potential benefits from criminal misconduct. Over the last two decades crime has become almost a way of life for both victims and victimizers, especially in the black community, and our misplaced eagerness to blame it all on environmental deprivation simply guarantees the perpetuation of our difficulties. Of course, the low-I.Q. thieves and hustlers who infest black neighborhoods are victims of their environment, but they are also its principal agents of victimization, and the problem is only going to be solved when their criminal tendencies are more effectively discouraged.

XV

OUR PRESENT WELFARE CRISIS

FINALLY, and most important, our welfare system seems almost a total failure. This system originated in the sixties with the laudable objective of ameliorating the poverty of blacks, but its principal accomplishment has been to expand welfare benefits to such an extent that a permanent underclass has been created primarily dependent upon its high birth rate to maximize its welfare benefits. Because our government furnishes substantial welfare payments (AFDC plus food stamps, a housing allowance, and Medicaid) on almost a blanket basis among single-parent families in ghetto areas, welfare has become the best guaranteed source of income for lower class black households, obliging nothing more than a steady sequence of pregnancies induced by temporary male companions who cannot be identified and held accountable for supporting their illegitimate children. Unrestrained reproduction has become the outstanding "natural resource" in these communities, and its cost to our government has become prohibitive in recent years,

AFDC alone having already amounted to 21.2 billion dollars in fiscal 1990. According to *Statistical Abstracts of U.S.: 1992*, our nation's combined welfare disbursements from federal, state and local sources adds up to 210.6 billion dollars, a rather large slice of our total government expenditures. Not all of this goes to blacks, of course, but if we can assume that at least one half of it does, this amounts to $3,500 per capita among the entire black population of the United States, not including the extra government costs for police work, education services, and the rest of the federal, state, and local infrastructure needed to help support and maintain order in the black community. Exactly how much is this total expense, and how much on a per capita basis? One can only guess.

Even more discouraging has been the demographic imbalance produced by our welfare largesse. Blacks have been reproducing to a disproportionate extent, at the annual average of 86.6 births per thousand in 1988, roughly two thirds of them outside of marriage. True, this high birth rate is now slightly dropping, but it remains significantly higher than the white average (63.0 per thousand) primarily because of the high fertility rate among poor black women—twice as high as among black women in the middle class (Taylor, pp. 288–89). From 1970 to 1990 the black population increased almost 15 percent according to official statistics, bringing their numbers up to 12.5 percent of the total population according to official tabulations including adjustments for undercount (Hacker, p. 15). This percentage can be expected to continue increasing on an exponential basis because of the AFDC lure and because a disproportionate share of blacks consists of children and young adults still in their fertile years. Moreover, mothers who are the most actively reproductive can be expected to encourage comparable tendencies in their children by the time they reach their mid-teens, both to imitate their mothers and to escape their crowded households by doing so. How can a lively young woman otherwise deficient in talent gain her immediate freedom from the drab, children-cluttered domicile of her mother? It is easy—by starting one of her own.

If present trends continue, we can therefore anticipate being confronted sooner or later with an enormous population of chronic "unemployables" as well as a comparable depletion of our national energies just feeding and policing this brand-new proletariat (according to this word's original Latin definition as state-sponsored "breeders"). Eventually our entire economy can be expected to suffer. Leon Bouvier, population consultant to President Carter's White House Commission on Immigration and Refugee Policy, predicted that at least half the U. S. population will be of black, Hispanic, and Asian origins within a hundred years [cited in Wilmot Robertson's angry book, *The Dispossessed Majority* (1981, pp. 65–66)]. This apparently inevitable trend can be absorbed by our economy if, and only if, this new population possesses the skills and incentives to assume a productive role alongside everybody else. However, our welfare system encourages an entirely different outcome by restricting its services to one-parent households on an incremental basis—the more children they procreate, the bigger their dole. Already results in the black community suggest both a biological and environmental nightmare, since mothers with the most desperate prospects for otherwise supporting themselves have been encouraged to raise the biggest families, unleashing upon our society a generation of children with virtually no chance of escaping their origins. Does anybody really believe that this underclass "minority" can continue to expand in this fashion without reducing the general standard of living for all of us? We cannot deceive ourselves that this dysgenic juggernaut is an open-ended privilege of democracy that can go on forever. It cannot. A revolutionary horde is being created right before our eyes, and its threat to our nation consists of nothing more than its perpetuating itself in exactly the same fashion as it is doing today. Its rapidly expanding leverage as an underclass comes from its total freedom to continue its activities without otherwise adjusting to the demands of white society. Welfare recipients need not hunt for jobs, or worry about their budget, or keep respectable hours, or pay their rent, or pay their doctors' bills. They can do as they please as long as they accept the inevitability of their marginal status. As already suggested in Chapter VII, Marxist theory has thus been turned on its head: This underclass has become the exploiters, everybody else the exploited, and the familiar metaphors of class conflict (theft, rape, the liquidation of the bourgeoisie, etc.) seem perversely appropriate. Thriving on the rhetoric of deprivation, our black underclass has so effectively stretched Judaeo-Christian charity that our culture will sooner or later be brought to its knees—perhaps within not more than three or four more generations. Foreign competitors such as Japan and western Europe need only sit back and patiently watch.

XVI

THE POLITICAL CONTEXT

WHAT COMPLICATES OUR RACIAL CRISIS is the fact that blacks have played a visible role in the history of our nation since its very beginning. The growth of our nation has been both directly and indirectly linked with the use of the black community by others. Black slaves accompanied the first Jamestown settlers in the early seventeenth century. The framing of the Constitution was only possible because slavery could be written into it at the demand of Georgia and South Carolina delegates in exchange for their support of the Connecticut Compromise. In the early nineteenth century the success of the cotton industry depended on an abundance of black slaves, thus giving our nation's agricultural interests, both north and south, enough leverage to counter-balance the expanding powers of bankers and industrialists from the northern states. But the need to eliminate slavery as a barbaric practice (as it was) justified the victory of these bankers and industrialists in the Civil War, by far the costliest blood-bath in our history, thus setting the stage for the robber barons and our modern industrial revolution. Only because of the slavery issue, therefore, were these financial interests afforded such a commanding position to forge their industrial empires without effective opposition from populist groups and constituencies. Down south, the crisis of the liberated black population led to the excesses of reconstruction, and then the restoration of white authority led to the excesses of an entrenched Democratic party oligarchy which dominated politics into the mid-twentieth century. At the turn of the twentieth century blacks provided a labor force for undesirable jobs and could occasionally be used as strikebreakers against the unions, again playing into the hands of the industrialists. After World War II, the steady migration of blacks from their tenant farms into our cities led to the problem of urban blight as we know it today. Of course, ghetto poverty existed before this immigration, but it was tame compared to present disintegrative trends which have left enormous "donut holes," mile-wide drug-jungles of gutted buildings at the center of most of our major cities. Then the urban riots of the sixties initiated the shift in social philosophy, giving us our hastily concocted Great Society programs which now seem to have created as many problems as they solved. Finally, the unwavering commitment of the liberal wing of the Democratic party to a continuation of these Great Society programs has effectively polarized our party system on a *de facto* racial basis, putting enough of a white majority in the Republican corner to guarantee an entrenched conservative leadership far more powerful than it would have been without the issue of black conciliation.

Though our nation's history has been disproportionately influenced by the racial issue, blacks themselves have been ineffective in representing their own interests. There have been notable exceptions, of course, but for the most part the primary impact of the black community in national politics has come from its sheer existence as an impoverished minority to be utilized at the discretion of others. "Cui bono?" (for whose advantage?), Cicero once asked, and the question obviously applies to the unintended services blacks have performed for interests otherwise opposed to them. At first the instrument of agrarian power against finance capital, our black minority quickly switched beneficiaries with the Civil War, and since then they have been trapped in their role unintentionally supportive of big business interests, first as strikebreakers and a cheap source of labor, now as a vocal minority whose demands have helped to drive the white lower-middle class, once the bastion of the Democratic party, into Republican ranks. Perversely, black slavery set the stage for the destruction of Jeffersonian democracy and delivered our nation's economy into the hands of finance capitalists for almost the entire five-decade period between the Civil War and World War I. Just as perversely, alliances once again shifted so that by the mid-1970's our progressive Democratic leadership so closely aligned itself with black voters that a white backlash has once again delivered our government into conservative hands. Without understanding its function, our black minority has consequently helped to keep Republican leadership in power for 84 of the last 132 years, almost two-thirds of the total, despite the ostensibly greater concern of our Democratic party leadership for the needs of the poor. If and when black anger further escalates against the white majority, this conservative trend can also be expected to escalate, and perhaps to dangerous levels after what seems destined to be another single-term interlude with a floundering liberal Democratic president.

XVII

WHAT IS TO BE DONE?

SO WHAT CAN BE DONE? How can our racial disparities be treated in a productive and civilized fashion? How can black living conditions be improved without further draining our economy? How can a solution be found that distributes costs and benefits on an equitable basis for all concerned? Exactly what kind of tide can be found that lifts all (or most) our boats, not just a few? Or should we reverse priorities and be looking into the virtues of triage, offering salvation to those who can be saved matched by benign neglect for the rest? How exactly can we find a balance to maximize the health and welfare of all our citizens, both black and white, on a truly realistic basis?

Not surprisingly, the first important step is to recognize the problem. If we are inexorably burdened with genetic racial differences in intelligence, it seems essential to acknowledge this division so we can deal with it more effectively. Any major bimodal disparity in cognitive ability can and should be recognized to be profoundly unfortunate, but if it exists, it does exist, and we must at least take into account its existence to be able to minimize its impact upon society. This disparity cannot disappear simply because we wish it out of consciousness, nor because we resort to bottomless federal spending and an unending parade of equal opportunity laws, programs, and special projects in order to impose solutions where they will not work. Sooner or later we must confront the awful truth that some blacks might be able to benefit from catch-up federal programs, but that many others will be just as immune to educational and job advancement as any Caucasian who suffers from comparable problems in cognitive deficiency. We must permit ourselves to recognize the probability that roughly 50 percent of our black population will be incompetent for tasks requiring cognitive skills in excess of an 85 I.Q., that roughly 84 percent of our black population will be incompetent for tasks requiring cognitive skills in excess of a 100 I.Q., and that at least 96 percent of our black population will be incompetent for the managerial and professional tasks requiring cognitive skills in excess of a 115 I.Q. To ignore this reality simply means wasted energy and frustration for all. Is my student, Lucinda, for example, any better able to express herself in writing now that she has completed my course in advanced expository writing? Does she have any more ideas to express that are worth communicating? Would advanced instruction toward an A.B., M.A., or, yes, even the Ph.D., be of any help? I doubt it. Like the unteachable Caucasian vendor, sweeper, or standby attendant whose place in society must be restricted to menial and obviously habitual assignments, the many blacks who suffer from a comparable I.Q. deficit should not be given tasks and responsibilities at any but the most basic level. We seem fully prepared to accept this necessity for disadvantaged whites; we must learn to accept it for the great majority of our black population. However, in the same spirit we must be prepared to accommodate those blacks who do possess the cognitive skills needed to participate in more challenging lines of work. Everything should be done to help them to establish their position in our society at levels appropriate to their full capability.

We cannot return to segregation—this would not only be repugnant but counterproductive as an apartheid invitation to social breakdown on a much more dangerous scale than before. Moreover, any retrogressive step in this direction would impose collective standards obviously unfair to the several million blacks fully competent to conduct their affairs on an equal basis with everybody else. However, a rigid commitment to equal opportunity seems just as dangerous. The collective standards now imposed by federal edict seem unfair to a large segment of our society, both black and white, and in the final analysis these standards betray the arrogance of trying to impose solutions through self-inflicted ignorance. It seems obvious that the best approach to our racial crisis today must include a cautious avoidance of all general panaceas, matched by a genuine democratic effort to deal with individual need as much as possible on an individual basis. Instead of quotas, "norms," and an army of ambitious federal bureaucrats who support themselves by penalizing their fellow citizens in the name of unachievable ideals, there should be a more restrained effort to ease improvements into existence with the least grief to the greatest number of people, and with an honest and objective recognition of genuine possibilities. Those who can make it should be encouraged; those who cannot, should not be. As with the eager but academically deficient black student who once told me he could not make up his mind whether to become a doctor, a judge, or a millionaire, individuals short on talent should be diplomatically assisted in toning down their level of expectations. Meanwhile, our current standards of performance should be retained, if not improved. The temptation should be resisted to compromise them any further in order to meet arbitrary racial percentage guidelines.

Academic programs which afford the education and placement of blacks on a realistic basis can be enthusiastically supported, since blacks with competitive intellectual skills should of course be given the needed training to let them compete on the job market for those positions they can fill. They should even be given compensatory assistance when appropriate, on the assumption that their contribution will eventually be the same as anybody else's. But other black students whose intelligence and academic performance persistently fall below acceptable standards should be steered as quickly and effectively as possible into job situations in which performance demands are less stringent. Many of these positions might seem unduly humiliating—such as in farm labor, dish washing, garbage collecting, and the like—but this problem does not seem to bother Hispanics at present (any more than it bothered me in my early twenties), and it should be no less bothersome to blacks. Little stigma is attached to these jobs in such countries as France, Germany, and Switzerland, where menial workers can be respected both for the essential services they perform and for their basic rights as tax-paying citizens. They have been tracked into jobs appropriate to their performance level on standardized tests administered to them throughout their primary and secondary schooling, and there is dignity afforded them as honest wage earners at least able and willing to support themselves gainfully. In comparable fashion, the United States needs to encourage the creation of many new basic labor positions on a nationwide scale through generous tax incentives to potential employers and through increased Federal aid to labor-intensive industries such as in the construction of highways and urban transit systems. The purpose of such tax incentives might seem unduly philanthropic to many Americans, but in fact the social benefits of providing jobs to unskilled labor are taken for granted throughout most of the rest of the world.

It also seems imperative to establish an effective birth control program for welfare mothers who exclusively support themselves by bearing great numbers of children. There are many more of these mothers than generally recognized, and their procreative excesses should not be permitted to impose on society a permanent problem exponentially dangerous to our future. Nobody benefits in the long run if our wealth and resources are taxed to the limit to support an underclass whose principal skill is in reproducing itself. The middle class will certainly suffer, but so will this underclass by sustaining a rate of growth in excess of the available income to spend on it. More inclusively, there has been a dysgenic catastrophe over the past three decades because the birth rate has dropped among whites, educated women, and middle and upper-class women at the same time as it has skyrocketed, respectively, among blacks, uneducated women, and women on welfare. In effect, the educated upper-middle class white female has stopped bearing her share of our population because of the burden and unacceptable cost of raising children in what she considers an appropriate fashion, while the uneducated black welfare mother bears as many children as she can because of free hospital costs and the expanded income guaranteed to her by raising additional children. If there is any social engineering intended in this remarkable demographic reversal, it is absolutely topsy-turvy and a guaranteed recipe for national disaster. Incentives exist, but only to make the wrong choices, and for everybody concerned. As a result, it seems urgent to reverse these incentives by encouraging motherhood among competent women able to raise children in a suitable manner while encouraging improved birth control practices and even abortions and sterilizations among chronic AFDC beneficiaries, if necessary by granting generous monetary awards. The easy availability of abortions helps to solve the problem with welfare mothers, but apparently at the expense of encouraging reduced fertility among middle and upper-middle class mothers. On the other hand, the criminalization of abortions might restore fertility rates for middle and upper-middle class mothers, but at the expense of even further increasing fertility rates among welfare mothers. Probably the best answer to the crisis would be to use financial incentives that offset each other: (a) by offering free abortions for all women as well as generous cash awards to welfare mothers for becoming sterilized after their first or second child; and (b) by offering free or cost-reduced obstetrics to all women and by granting a generous *proportional* tax deduction for each dependent child, thus encouraging the use of children as tax shelters among those whose income is high enough both to benefit from such an arrangement and to raise children in relatively prosperous circumstances. The cost of implementing such measures on a nationwide scale might seem prohibitive, but, once adjusted, it would be negligible compared to the financial burden we can expect if current population trends continue on their present course.

Catholic and fundamentalist Protestant opposition can, of course, be expected against any government policy that features abortion and sterilization, but a misplaced commitment to religious ideals cannot be permitted to impose consequences entirely at odds with the benefits of civilization we presently take for granted. The tiny foetus is a miracle beyond all comprehension, but its proliferation should not be so indiscriminately promoted that untold numbers of its kind are born into this world only to grow up as pimps and prostitutes, muggers, burglars, and welfare mothers dedicated to expanding the cycle until our entire culture is brought to its knees. The extremist defense of each and every potentially fertilized ovum as a future citizen with full constitutional privileges cannot be permitted to destroy our nation as we know it today.

As for dealing with the crime rate, it seems obvious that our bimodal society has produced bimodal results and that most of the conventional wisdom which has been dredged up about the apprehension, prosecution, and rehabilitation of the white criminal simply does not apply to the underclass black criminal—at least not in the same way, or to the same extent. We seem to be trying to abide by Eurocentric legal guarantees in a third-world situation, and results have been less than satisfactory. Some compromise must therefore be found to adjust the defense of our civil rights to fit the special problems of lawlessness in our black community. There must be a more concerted effort to keep police officers on the sidewalks in crime-ridden neighborhoods, and any disrespect or violence against these officers must be treated with commensurate severity. As much as possible, black and white officers must be used as teams in these neighborhoods. A full inquiry must be undertaken for any reported felony even when it seems obvious that no arrests can be made. Neighbors and potential suspects must be questioned, and, in the event that arrests can be made, multiple offenders must not be permitted to negotiate for reduced sentences. Crime-prone youngsters must be identified as early as possible and steered into socially acceptable activities (for example, sports, dance, and dramatic productions) in which they can productively express their feelings without committing themselves to more destructive kinds of behavior. In other words, a complex multi-dimensional strategy is needed to reduce the crime rate which presently exists in the black community, and if such a program obliges a bigger budget we must be prepared to absorb such a burden in the taxes we pay. Why? Because each ghetto crime successfully committed advertises the profit and excitement of this kind of behavior, thus spawning more criminal acts of its kind, and if these too prove to be successful (as they usually do), lawlessness quickly gets out of control. On the other hand, each criminal investigation that leads to arrests and imprisonment helps to keep the crime rate down by discouraging similar criminal behavior by others. Exemplification plays a disproportionate role, obliging a more stringent commitment to law enforcement than might otherwise seem necessary. Paradoxically, the more effective the criminal justice apparatus, the less it will be needed. Only if rigid guidelines are imposed can our legal system be relaxed without encouraging another crime wave.

Obviously whites stand to benefit from a major reduction in black crime, but the principal beneficiaries would be the blacks themselves, since they constitute the majority of its victims, and, just as important, since the flagrant misbehavior of black criminals can mostly be blamed for white prejudice against the black community. Each group of young offenders who shuffle along sidewalks looking for trouble act as a walking electric billboard telling the world of the potential threat of blacks against everybody else. Not more than fifteen or twenty of these young malefactors thrown into a neighborhood can initiate white flight and shift white buying patterns from downtown stores to shopping malls safely located elsewhere. As products of AFDC, Medicaid, compensatory educational treatment, and the generous criminal justice system, these maladjusted teenagers have become the soldiers of the ghetto, but their victories are entirely Pyrrhic—they spread failure and poverty wherever they turn. Any triumphs they obtain at the expense of "the man" only redound to the greater misery of the black community as a whole. They must consequently be steered into more productive activities, and those who refuse to accept this guidance by breaking the law must be swiftly incarcerated—partly to encourage their rehabilitation, partly to keep them off the streets until they reach a more responsible age, and partly to discourage criminal behavior by others.

The point I am trying to make regarding black deprivation in the areas of jobs, education, welfare, and crime control is that most improvements will depend upon the recognition that our society is up against an intractable bimodal distribution in I.Q. big enough to oblige a somewhat different social approach. As indicated earlier, our standards must be held the same, but new types of social modification must be encouraged based on realistic bimodal expectations. This differentiation must be flexible enough to take into account those individuals who can fend for themselves, but for others it must be used to the extent that it is needed. Of course, full political equality must be extended to everybody regardless of race, sex, or creed, but all programs of social modification must be better conceived to adjust expectations to the performance levels which are truly possible—from each according to his ability, to each according to his need.

Our problem today is that any program based on the recognition of separate ability levels would be strenuously rejected by almost the entire liberal establishment. Most of our leading journalists and social scientists have effectively brainwashed themselves as well as those who attend their classes and read their books and articles into taking for granted the improbable evolutionary assumption that every race shares exactly the same cognitive potential as every other race regardless of differences in the climate of origin, regardless of countless anatomical differences, regardless of significant craniometric differences, and regardless of repeatedly confirmed differences in I.Q. testing. Their line of reasoning is based on the premise that observed differences in behavior cannot be submitted to qualitative comparison because they result from different cultural backgrounds. No normative distinctions may be entertained except, of course, in rejecting the "racist" viciousness of those who succumb to this temptation. Let anybody utter his slightest doubts about the validity of their egalitarian faith, and immediately these Samaritans vent upon him their full wrath for his presumed bigotry. And, indeed, some of their assumptions are true. It is to be granted that primitive cultures can be very sophisticated indeed, that our white power structure has been oppressive in its treatment of blacks, and even that many blacks possess much more cognitive potential than is ever fully realized. However, this does not mean that black I.Q. averages are the same as for whites or that blacks with low I.Q.'s are able to compete with anybody else in jobs that demand superior intellectual achievement. Any effort to support these claims despite incontrovertible evidence to the contrary is entirely tendentious and deserves to be treated as such. The motivation behind such an effort is undoubtedly benevolent, but this does not mitigate the responsibility of our liberal propagandists for the basic distortions they promulgate or for the social harm produced by our general acceptance of these distortions. As long as their campaign enjoys almost universal support among intellectuals there is little that can be done about the very serious racial problems we are now up against. Blacks will continue to be angry that they are being deprived of their just desserts; whites will continue to take flight; and expensive social programs that aggravate the crisis will continue to be hatched and enforced. Meanwhile, the needed modifications will just as effectively be excluded from consideration for their presumed racist bigotry. More of the same has become our credo, exactly when *less*, or *different*, is so desperately needed.

I myself would be delighted if no I.Q. differences existed to the disadvantage of blacks. It would be a genuine pleasure to be able to say of blacks, as I can of Jews and Orientals, that, if anything, their cognitive skills are at least equal to those of Caucasians, so the great majority of them can be expected to make a significant positive contribution to our society once the programs now in existence bring their performance levels fully in line with the rest of us. I would even be prepared to endure further decades of disruptive social engineering to make it come true. However, there is too much evidence to the contrary. There are too many student failures, too many senselessly violent crimes, too many professional welfare mothers, too many incompetent employees, and too many enclaves of underclass misery to be able to predict anything except the inexorable worsening of our present crisis unless we act soon to make a few basic changes in our national strategy. Unfortunately, American civilization hangs in the balance. We can either deal with the problem on a realistic basis or we can cling to our official mythology until the problem gets so completely out of hand that the rhetoric of racial conflict finally gains its bloody realization. The choice is ours, and its overwhelming importance is to be measured by our very desperate refusal to confront it.

REFERENCES

Achebe, C. *Things Fall Apart*. New York: Astor-Honor, 1959.

Baker, J. R. *Race*. New York: Oxford University Press, 1974.

Beals, K. L., Smith, C. L., and Dodd, S. M. Brain size, cranial morphology, climate and time machines. *Current Anthropology*, 1984, 25, 301–330.

Blits, J., and Gottfredson, L. Equality or lasting inequality? *Transaction/SOCIETY,* 1990, 27, 4–11.

Blits, J., and Gottfredson, L. Employment testing and job performance. *The Public Interest*, 1990, 98, 18–25.

Bouchard, T. J., Lykken, D., and McGue, M. Sources of human psychological differences: The Minnesota study of twins reared apart. *Science*, 1990, 250, 223–8.

Broman, S. H., Nichols, P. I., and Kennedy, W. A. *Retardation in Young Children*. Hillsdale, N. J.: Lawrence Erlbaum, 1987.

Cain, D. P., and Vanderwolf, C. H. A critique of Rushton on race, brain size, and intelligence. *Personality and Individual Differences*, 1990, 11, 777–84.

Carothers, J. C. *The Mind of Man in Africa*. London: The Garden City Press, Ltd., 1972.

125

Connolly, C. J. *External Morphology of the Primate Brain.* Springfield, Ill.: C. C. Thomas, 1950.

Davis, B. Neo-Lysenkoism, I.Q. and the press. *The Public Interest,* Fall 1983.

Edsall, T. B., and Edsall, M. D. *Chain Reaction: The Impact of Race, Rights, and Taxes on American Politics.* New York: W. W. Norton, Inc., 1991.

Eells, K., Davis, A., Havighurst, R. J., Herrick, V. E., and Tyler, R. W. *Intelligence and Cultural Differences.* Chicago: University of Chicago Press, 1951.

Epstein, R. A. *Forbidden Grounds: The Case Against Employment Discrimination Laws.* Cambridge, Mass.: Harvard University Press, 1992.

Eysenck, H. J. *The Inequality of Man.* San Diego: EDITS Publishers, 1973.

Eysenck, H. J. *A Model for Intelligence.* Bolin: Springer-Verlag, 1982.

Forbath, P. *The River Congo.* New York: Harper and Row, 1977.

Fynn, H. R. *The Diary of Henry Francis Fynn.* Edited by J. Stuart. Pietermaritzburg: Shooter and Shooter, 1950.

Gallais, P., and Planques, L. *Med. Trop.,* 1951, II, 5–32.

Garrett, H. E. The equalitarian dogma. *Perspectives in Biology and Medicine,* Summer 1961, 4, 480–484.

Gordon, C. C. et al. *1988 Anthropometric Survey of U. S. Army Personnel: Summary Statistics Interim Report.* Natick, Mass.: U. S. Army Natick Research, Development and Engineering Center, 1988.

Gottfredson, L. The g factor in employment: A special issue of the *Journal of Vocational Behavior,* 1986, 29. [Including articles by A. R. Jensen, R. L. Thorndike, J. Hunter, L. Gottfredson, L. Gottfredson and J. Crouse, and J. Hawks].

Gould, S. J. *The Mismeasure of Man.* New York: Norton, 1981.

Gould, S. J. Who has donned Lysenko's mantle? *The Public Interest*, Spring 1984, 148–151.

Hacker, A. *Two Nations: Black and White, Separate, Hostile, Unequal.* New York: Charles Scribner's Sons, 1992.

Harnad, S., editor. Precis of bias in mental testing. *The Behavioral and Brain Sciences*, 1980, 3, 325.

Herrnstein, R. J. I.Q. *The Atlantic Monthly*, September 1971.

Herrnstein, R. J. *IQ in the Meritocracy*. Boston: Little, Brown, & Company, 1973.

Herrnstein, R. J. IQ testing and the media. *The Atlantic Monthly*, August 1982.

Ho, K-c., Roessmann, U., Straumfjord, J. V., and Monroe, G. Analysis of brain weight: I. Adult brain weight in relation to sex, race, and age. *Archives of Pathology and Laboratory Medicine*, 1980, 104, 635–639.

Ho, K-c., Roessmann, U., Straumfjord, J. V., and Monroe, G. Analysis of brain weight: II. Adult brain weight in relation to body height, weight, and surface area. *Archives of Pathology and Laboratory Medicine*, 1980, 104, 640–645.

Ho, K-c., Roessmann, U., Hause, L., and Monroe, G. Newborn brain weight in relation to maturity, sex, and race. *Annals of Neurology*, 1981, 10, 243–246.

Ho, H-z, Baker, L. A., and Decker, S. N. Covariation between intelligence and speed of cognitive processing: Genetic and environmental influences. *Behavior Genetics.* 1988, 18, 247–261.

Hulse, F. S. *The Human Species: An Introduction to Physical Anthropology*. New York: Random House, 1963.

Huntington, E. *Civilization and Climate*, 3rd ed. New Haven: Yale University Press, 1924.

Huntington, E. *The Character of Races*. New York: Scribner's, 1925.

Jefferson, T. Notes on the State of Virginia, in *Writings*. New York: The Library of America, 1984.

Jencks, C. *Rethinking Social Policy*. Cambridge, Mass.: Harvard University Press, 1992.

Jensen, A. R. Social class, race, and genetics: Implications for education. *American Educational Research Journal*, 1968, 5(1), 1–42.

Jensen, A. R. *Bias in Mental Testing*. New York: The Free Press, 1980.

Jensen, A. R. *Straight Talk about Mental Tests*. New York: Macmillan, 1981.

Jensen, A. R. The debunking of scientific fossils and straw persons. *Contemporary Education Review*, Summer 1982, 121–35.

Jensen, A. R. Reaction Time and Psychometric g, in H. J. Eysenck, ed. *A Model for Intelligence*. Bolin: Springer-Verlag, 1982.

Jensen, A. R. The nature of the black-white difference on various psychometric tests: Spearman's hypothesis. *Behavioral and Brain Sciences*, 1985, 8, 193–263.

Jensen, A. R. g: Artifact or reality? *Journal of Vocational Behavior*, 1986, 29, 301–31.

Jensen, A. R. Further evidence for Spearman's hypothesis concerning black-white differences on psychometric tests. *Behavioral and Brain Sciences*, 1987, 10, 512–19.

Jensen, A. R., and Figueroa, R. A. Forward and backward digit span interaction with race and IQ: Prediction from Jensen's theory. *Journal of Educational Psychology*, 1975, 67, 882–893.

Jensen, A. R., and Sinha, S. N. Physical Correlates of Human Intelligence. In P. A. Vernon, ed., *Biological Approaches to the Study of Human Intelligence*. Norwood, N. J.: Ablex, 1991.

Kemp, L. C. D. Environmental and other characteristics determining attainments in primary schools. *British Journal of Educational Psychology*, 1955, 25, 66–77.

Klineberg, O. *Negro Intelligence and Selective Migration.* New York: Columbia University Press, 1935.

Klineberg, O. (Editor) *Characteristics of the American Negro.* New York: Harper, 1944.

Lamb, D. *The Africans.* New York: Random House, 1982.

Lehmann, N. *The Promised Land: The Great Black Migration and How It Changed America.* New York: Alfred A. Knopf, 1991.

Levin, M. Implications of race and sex differences for compensatory affirmative action and the concept of discrimination. *The Journal of Social, Political and Economic Studies*, 1990, 15, 175–212.

Levin, M. Race differences: An overview. *The Journal of Social, Political and Economic Studies*, 1991, 16, 195–216.

Levin, M. Responses to race differences in crime. *Journal of Social Philosophy*, 1992, 23, 5–29.

Loehlin, J. C., Lindzey, G., and Spuhler, J. N. *Race Differences in Intelligence.* San Francisco: Freeman, 1975.

Lynn, R. New evidence in brain size and intelligence: A comment on Rushton and Cain and Vanderwolf. *Personality and Individual Differences*, 1990, 11, 795–97.

Lynn, R. Race differences in brain size and intelligence: A global perspective. *The Mankind Quarterly*, 1991, 31, 255–96.

Lynn, R. The evolution of racial differences in intelligence. *The Mankind Quarterly*, 1991, 32, 99–121.

Montague, M. F. A. Intelligence of northern Negroes and southern whites in the First World War. *American Journal of Psychology*, 1945, 58, 161–188.

Murray, C. *Losing Ground: American Social Policy 1950–1980.* New York: Basic Books, Inc., 1984.

Naipaul, S. *North of South.* New York: Penguin, 1980.

Naipaul, V. S. *A Bend in the River.* New York: Knopf, 1979.

Naipaul, V. S. A New King for the Congo: Mobutu and the Nihilism of Africa. In *The Return of Eva Peron.* New York: Knopf, 1980.

Osborne, R. T. *Twins: Black and White*. Athens, Ga.: Foundation for Human Understanding, 1980.

Osborne, R. T., and McGurk, F. C. J., editors. *The Testing of Negro Intelligence*, volume 2. Athens, Ga.: Foundation for Human Understanding, 1982.

Pearl, R. Weight of the Negro brain. *Science*, 1934, 80, 431–434.

Pearson, R. *Race, Intelligence, and Bias in Academe*. With an introduction by Hans Eysenck. Washington, D. C.: Scott-Townsend Publishers, 1991.

Robertson, W. *The Dispossessed Majority*, revised edition. Cape Canaveral: Howard Allen, 1981.

Rosenthal, R., and Jacobson, L. *Pygmalion in the Classroom*. New York: Holt, Rinehart and Winston, 1968.

Roth, B. Social psychology's "Racism." *Public Interest*, 1990, 98, 26–36.

Rushton, J. P. Race differences in behavior: A review and evolutionary analysis. *Personality and Individual Differences*, 1988, 9, 1009–1024.

Rushton, J. P. The reality of racial differences: A rejoinder with new evidence. *Personality and Individual Differences*, 1988, 9, 1035–40.

Rushton, J. P. Race differences in sexuality and their correlates: Another look and physiological models. *Journal of Research in Personality*, 1989, 23, 35–54.

Rushton, J. P. Race, brain size, and intelligence: A reply to Cernovsky. *Psychological Reports*, 1990, 66, 659–66.

Rushton, J. P. Race, brain size and intelligence: A rejoinder to Cain and Vanderwolf. *Personality and Individual Differences*, 1990, 11, 785–94.

Rushton, J. P. Race, brain size, and intelligence: Another reply to Cernovsky. *Psychological Reports*, 1991, 68, 500–02.

Rushton, J. P. Do r-K strategies underlie human race differences? A reply to Weizmann et al. *Canadian Psychology*, 1991, 32, 29–42.

Rushton, J. P. Cranial capacity related to sex, rank, and race in a stratified random sample of 6,325 U. S. military personnel. *Intelligence*, 1992, 16, 401–13.

Rushton, J. P., and Bogaert, A. F. Race differences in sexual behavior: Testing an evolutionary hypothesis. *Journal of Research in Personality*, 1987, 21, 529–557.

Rushton, J. P., and Bogaert, A. F. Race versus social class differences in sexual behavior: A follow-up test of the r/K dimension. *Journal of Research in Personality*, 1988, 22, 249–272.

Seligman, D. *A Question of Intelligence*. New York: Birch Lane, 1992.

Shuey, A. *The Testing of Negro Intelligence*, 2nd edition. New York: Social Science Press, 1966.

Silberman, C. *Criminal Violence, Criminal Justice*. New York: Random, 1978.

Simmons, K. Cranial capacities by both plastic and water techniques with cranial linear measurements of the reserve collection; white and Negro. *Human Biology*, 1942, 473–498.

Snyderman, M., and Rothman, S. *The IQ Controversy, The Media and Public Policy*. New Brunswick, N. J.: Transaction Books, 1988.

Spearman, C. *The Nature of "Intelligence" and the Principles of Cognition*. London: Macmillan, 1923.

Tainter, J. A. *The Collapse of Complex Societies*. New York: Cambridge University Press, 1988.

Taylor, J. *Paved with Good Intentions*. New York: Carroll and Graf, 1992.

Todd, T. W. Cranial capacity and linear dimensions in white and Negro. *American Journal of Physical Anthropology*, 1923, 6, 97–194.

Van Valen, L. Brain size and intelligence in man. *American Journal of Physical Anthropology*, 1974, 40, 417–23.

Vernon, P. *Intelligence: Heredity and Environment*. San Francisco: Freeman, 1979.

Vernon, P. A. The heritability of measures of speed of information-processing. *Personality and Individual Differences*, 1989, 10, 573–576.

Vincent, Ken R. Black/white IQ differences: Does age make the difference? *Journal of Clinical Psychology*, 1991, 47, 266–70.

Vint, F. W. A preliminary note on the cell content of prefrontal cortex of East African natives. *East African Medical Journal*, 1932, 9, 30–55.

Vint, F. W. The brain of the Kenya native. *Journal of Anatomy*, 1934, 68, 216–23.

Westermann, D. *The African Today and Tomorrow*. London: Oxford University Press, 1939.

Wigdor, A. K., and Garner, W. R. *Ability Testing: Uses, Consequences, and Controversies. Part I: Report of the Committee*. Washington, D. C.: National Academy Press, 1982.

Wigdor, A. K., and Garner, W. R. *Ability Testing: Uses, Consequences, and Controversies. Part 2: Documentation Section*. Washington, D. C.: National Academy Press, 1982.

Willerman, L., Shultz, R., Rutledge, J. N., and Bigler, E. Magnetic Resonance Imaged Brain Structures and Intelligence. Paper presented at the 19th Annual Meeting of the Behavior Genetics Association, Charlottesville, Virginia, June 8–11, 1989.

Williams, C. D. Child health in the Gold Coast. *The Lancet*, 1938, 234, 97–102.

Wilson, J. Q., and Herrnstein, R. *Crime and Human Nature*. New York: Simon and Schuster, 1985.

Wilson, W. J. *The Truly Disadvantaged*. Chicago: University of Chicago Press, 1987.